SLAYING THE GIANTS OF

DOMESTIC VIOLENCE

FINDING MY DAVID IN A MAN CALLED JESUS

DR. CAROL L. H. JONES

green house
PUBLISHING AGENCY

SLAYING THE GIANTS OF DOMESTIC VIOLENCE: FINDING MY DAVID IN A MAN CALLED JESUS by Dr. Carol L. H. Jones

Published by GreeneHouse Publishing Agency, LLC |
www.greenehousepublishingagency.com

1129 Weaver Diary Rd. #17134, Chapel Hill, NC 27516

Unless otherwise identified, Scripture quotations are taken from the King James Version and Chronological Life Application Study Bible.

Visit the author's website at www.illuminatedexpressions.com and www.thecenterforcounselingcoachingeducation.com

ISBN: (13) 978-0-9796366-5-3

Printed in the United States of America

DEDICATION

To Jermaine, Christopher, and Benjamin. As I looked into the promises of God it was because of you that I wanted to be better and do better. To create a legacy in Christ Jesus that you would want to pass on to your children for a thousand generations. Thank you, my loves.

Forever and always,
Mom

ABOUT THE LOGO

From this experience and through the writing of this book, the Lord gave me the words of the "logo". I have created a symbol of hope to represent domestic violence. A symbol around which we can all unite to send a definitive message loud and clear: that there is Life After Domestic Violence!

No more death of hopes, dreams, and futures. Thank you for believing with me and supporting me as we all come together to shift the landscape of and bring an end to Domestic Violence.

TABLE OF CONTENTS

INTRODUCTION

From biblical times, the name Goliath has been associated with events in life that are frightening and overwhelming. In this book, the comparison to Goliath represents things that seem to be just too big to manage. Domestic violence (DV) is such an experience.

I'm using the biblical story of David and Goliath to demonstrate how overwhelming and daunting domestic violence can be in the lives of victims, family members of victims, friends of victims, and even to the entire community. Domestic violence is not *her, his, or their* problem. Domestic violence is *everyone's* problem. As Goliath was a threat to all of Israel, so domestic violence is a threat to an entire community, city, state, and nation.

When victims decide to leave abusers and destroy the giants of fear and abuse in their lives by standing up and saying no more, things can [and usually do] become dangerous. Abusers tend to become even more abusive when their victims try to leave, often even violent.

A domestic violence victim's choice to leave is not always celebrated. In addition to the abuser, there will likely be others who may become angry, jealous, or feel threatened by the victim's choice to leave.

Illustrated in the pages of this book, through the story of David and Goliath, are examples of how abusers or batterers position themselves in the lives of victims. Also illustrated are scenarios of how victims' resolve can be broken down over time. How abusers systematically work to weaken their victims, making them more vulnerable to fear and manipulation, in order to keep the peace or keep from being hurt or killed. As scenes are described from the story of David and Goliath, I will cross-reference them with the abuser-victim relationship.

My hope is that through the examples depicted, readers will come to understand how abusers establish emotional, mental, and physical holds on their victims. I also discuss the role others may play in the relationship between victims and abusers and how their involvement may help or hurt the victim.

This book describes abusers. How they, like Goliath, position themselves in the lives of victims. The tactics abusers use are explained, along with what happens when Goliath meets David, who trusted in God to defend him against the giant. We all face Goliath-sized situations and problems that appear too big to handle or are too overwhelming to overcome. Despite what your Goliath might look or sound like, don't be discouraged. Read on and find out what David did, and how he conquered the giant.

Chapter 1
THE NOISE IN MY HEAD

I remember the scream. I screamed so loud the sound reverberated off the walls of my skull and gave me a headache. I yelled and yelled but no one came. In my mind's eye, I could see a swarm of people rushing to the vehicle and pulling him from the van, while others made sure my baby and I were safe.

The mob pushed him to the ground and demanded to know why he had hurt me. Yet as I sat there shocked and confused, with my head and face throbbing from the pain, no one heard me scream, and no one came to my rescue. We, (I was behind the wheel) drove away in silence, leaving that spot behind, but the incident was forever etched in my mind. I left there and pretended, as I had so many times before, that nothing had happened. But in my head, the screaming would not stop.

As I drove away, I wondered where the military police were. They had stopped us on that same stretch of road before. I thought that surely they had seen what had happened as they patrolled the area. But, on that day, they were nowhere to be found.

The pain! I remembered the pain and how much my face and the side of my head hurt. It happened as I drove our family van home with our two-year-old son in his car seat behind me. My abuser, sitting in the passenger seat, had punched me in the face. That was the last time I remember being hit, and that was also the blow that marked the end of our relationship.

I wanted my marriage to work, I wanted my children to grow up with their father, and I wanted him to love us and treat us right. But no matter what I did, he remained a tyrant who would not be stopped. He was my Goliath. Fear of him was a giant in my life. I knew I had to rid myself of him, and of the fear of him, if I wanted to live. If I wanted my children to have anything that resembled a normal life, I had to leave him. He had become my Goliath, and I needed a David to set me, and eventually us, free!

For years, I tried to find the courage and the words to describe my experiences. Friends would say, you should write a book. But what would I say? How could I ever describe the pain and terror that I lived with in my mind, body, heart, and soul, for so many years? How could I put the words onto paper for the world to read without hurting my children and exposing my most vulnerable self?

While reading the story of David and Goliath in the Bible, God gave me a revelation that helped me describe how domestic violence has taken individuals and societies captive. I ask you to Read on! My prayer is that the words within these pages would be the catalyst to help set you and those you love free. Blessings, your humble servant.

Simple Choices Astronomical Consequences

How could such a simple choice, such as going on a date with someone or falling in love, end up having such dire consequences? Has this thought ever crossed your mind? Have you been plagued with thoughts and feelings of guilt that says, "If only I had not gone out with that person?" When I read the story of King Saul, I wondered how one decision could cost someone so much.

Before moving forward, I need to set the stage and provide a bit of background to help you understand the story being told. In the biblical story of David and Goliath, there are several characters who stand out as central figures. Saul, the King; David, the Shephard boy; Samuel, the Prophet; Eliab, the soldier and David's brother; and Goliath, the Giant.

Let me start at the beginning. Saul was chosen as the first king of Israel. The people of Israel were God's chosen people. Samuel was the prophet at the time, and he was responsible for giving instructions from the Lord to the king. In 1 Samuel 15, God instructed Saul [through Samuel] to completely destroy the Amalekites. During the time of King Saul, when God gave the command to destroy a nation, that is exactly what He meant. Saul mobilized his army and went to fight against the Amalekites. However, he decided to keep the best the Amalekites had—sheep, goats, etc.—and even spared the king's life. Because of that choice, God rejected Saul from being king.

God viewed Saul's decision as disobedience, which was unacceptable. In that same chapter, there is an explanation of how God viewed Saul's decision. The prophet Samuel told King Saul that "to obey is better than sacrifice, and to harken better than the fat of rams." The next verse goes on to say, "For rebellion is as the sin of witchcraft, and stubbornness is as iniquity and idolatry. Because thou hast rejected the word of the Lord, He hath also rejected thee from being king (1 Samuel 15:22-23)."

Now you might think, "Wait a minute." "You mean to tell me that just because this man chose not to obey God, God took the entire kingdom away from him?" Yes! That is exactly what happened, but it did not happen overnight. Quite some time passed between the time when Saul disobeyed God and when the kingdom was lost.

God is serious about obedience. Why? Because obedience is for our protection and the protection of those we love. We have an example of obedience in Christ Jesus, who was so obedient that He died for you and me.

Saul, realizing his mistake, said to Samuel, "I have sinned and transgressed the commandments of the Lord." Saul went on to tell Samuel that he did what he did because he had listened to and obeyed the voice of the people. Saul blamed the people, saying that listening to the voice of the people caused him to disobey God's voice. On that day, Saul lost his anointing as king, along with the Spirit and strength of God that had previously been with him. These were replaced by a spirit of fear and a tormenting spirit.

Like Saul, I have had instances where I did not do the right thing. I can think of several occasions and situations where I was disobedient and things did not go well for me. As a result of my choices, I was hurt emotionally and physically. In other situations, I could have lost my life. Also, I trusted others who I did not think would hurt me, but they did.

Maybe you believe, either as a result of your own guilt or because of words spoken by others, that the abuse is your fault and a consequence of your choices. Some individuals who hold that belief often follow the old adage, "You made your bed hard. Now lie in it." When referring to domestic violence, that couldn't be further from the truth. God loves us and wants us to follow his word for our protection. But when we do not follow his word, it in no way *causes* abuse.

It is important to reflect on and understand the impact of your choices. Just like understanding Saul's position at this point in the story will provide you with a picture of why things happened the way they did later in the story.

Chapter 2
YOUR POSITION MATTERS

As the king of Israel, Saul faced opponents from outside his kingdom who sought their destruction. Before he faced Goliath, Saul's position was important because it demonstrated several things. He had lost the Spirit of God, and it had been replaced with a tormenting spirit. Saul's relationship with God provides a great lesson for us. Where we are spiritually, emotionally, and mentally has a lot to do with how we: a) face, b) respond to, or c) handle the giants of life. God watched over and protected his people, the children of Israel. God's Spirit is that of wisdom, strength, and truth. When we walk in and with God's Spirit, we are protected and blessed.

Throughout this book, I will challenge you to stop, do a self-examination, and engage in self-reflection to assist you with moving forward. Think for a moment about when you met your abuser. What was your emotional, mental, and spiritual state? Please note that these moments of self-examination and self-reflection are not meant to cast blame or guilt upon you. I am asking you to take the time to remember who you were before. . . before the abuse.

Prayer Point: Father, my prayer is that you would lead your child in obedience to your word, that she or he would be in position to receive your blessings in Jesus' name, Amen. The story continues.

King Saul and David the Shephard Boy

In 1 Samuel chapter 16, God spoke to Samuel and asked him how long he would mourn for Saul, seeing as God had rejected him from reigning over Israel. Samuel loved Saul, and it grieved him that Saul chose to be disobedient to God, and that God had rejected him. God told Samuel to fill his horn with oil. He was going to send him to Jesse the Bethlehemite because He (God) had chosen a king from among Jesse's sons. In chapter 16, verse 2, Samuel asked God how he could go to Bethlehem to anoint a king, when, if Saul heard of what he was doing, Saul would kill him. God's response to Samuel was to take a heifer (a young female cow) with him and say he was going to make a sacrifice to the Lord.

Prayer Point: It is so important to express our fears and concerns to God when he calls or sends us to complete a mission. God's response to our problems will always satisfy the problem at hand.

God told Samuel to call Jesse to the sacrifice and He would show Samuel what to do and who to anoint when he got there. Samuel did as God commanded, and went to Jesse's house. When he arrived in Bethlehem, the elders of the town trembled at his coming and asked if he came peaceably. And he said peaceably. He told the men why he was there and called Jesse and his sons to the sacrifice.

When they came, Samuel looked at Jesse's sons and said to God, "Surely you have chosen Eliab." But God had not. God told him not to look on

Eliab's countenance or on the height of his stature because, "I have refused him. For the Lord seeth not as man seeth; for man looketh on the outward appearance but the Lord looketh on the heart."

> I would like to interject something at this point. God looks at our hearts. He knows exactly why we do what we do and the purpose and desire behind every decision we make. God sees into the depths of our hearts and souls. We cannot hide from Him.

As victims of abuse, how many times have others looked at your abuser and commented on how handsome, nice, or sweet he or she appears to be? What these people do not know and cannot see is your abuser's heart. Those making such comments do not know the darkness and deception that you alone see and live with each day. They know nothing of the heart that is filled with anger and rage. They look at you from the outside and judge *you* because you have a problem with him or her.

Prayer Point: God loves you and knows you and wants the best for you despite what you might have been told. Father, I pray you will open my understanding and my spiritual eyes that I may see myself as you see me. In Jesus' name, Amen.

When it comes to judgment, God does not use the same measurement as we use.

Seven of Jesse's sons passed before Samuel, and God did not choose any of them. Then Samuel asked Jesse, "Are all your children here? Jesse said, "No, my youngest keepeth the sheep." Samuel told Jesse to fetch him. In 1 Samuel 16, Samuel anointed David in the presence of his brothers, and the scripture says. "…and the Spirit of the Lord came upon David from that day forward."

Numbers 27 contains a relevant comparison to the story in 1 Samuel. It says, "And the Lord said unto Moses take thee Joshua the son of Nun, a man in whom is the Spirit and lay thine hand upon him." Moses had asked God to appoint a leader, and that verse was God's response to his request. Numbers 27:16:-says, "Let the Lord, the God of the spirits of all flesh, set a man over the congregation."

God commands the spirits, and we have no life without God, who gives us breath. The same Spirit that was in Joshua came upon David. And that same Spirit is available to us today to lead God's people and do His will. After the Spirit of the Lord left Saul, his servants recognized that an evil spirit often came upon him and recommended finding a skillful musician to play for him when the spirit troubled him, so he could get relief.

Someone recommended David as being good on the harp, and Saul called for him. When Saul saw David, he loved him and made him his armor bearer. God had promoted David, moving him from the fields minding the sheep to the king's palace and into the king's army as his armor bearer. Saul had no idea he had just sent for his replacement.

Prayer Point: God, I know that I cannot see beyond my current situation, but I trust that you do. Give me the faith, Father, to see a way out of this abusive relationship. I cannot change my abuser, nor can I save my marriage on my own. Show me the way, Lord, in Jesus' name, Amen.

Note: If you are an abuser reading this book, I want you to know that God loves you too. God can and will help you. If you want to be helped. God can help you stop abusing your partner. Most importantly, God can help you stop abusing yourself through guilt, shame, and condemnation. Trust and believe in Him. If we confess our sins, he is faithful and just to forgive us our sins and to cleanse us from all unrighteousness (1 John 1:9).

Seek help from a skilled professional (counselor, therapist, psychologist, or psychiatrist), or join a batterer's prevention program. Help is available to everyone who wants it. All you need to do is ask.

When the evil spirit came upon Saul, David took his harp and played, and Saul was refreshed. Then the evil spirit departed. The Bible says Saul loved David greatly and asked Jesse if David could stay with him. When I think of all the dynamics involved, and how God orchestrated everything as He did and how He commands the universe, it is mind-altering. God, in His infinite wisdom, can change your situation practically overnight.

Now David stood before the king of Israel, who no longer had the Spirit of God. Saul had called for David, a shepherd boy who had the Spirit of God, and neither one of them fully understood what was going on. As I consider what I've learned and now know from the Bible, it is the Spirit of God that allows us to lead lives that are pleasing to Him. It is His Spirit that moves us to obedience so that we do not fulfill the lust of the flesh. Yes, we can override the Spirit of God with our own selfish will because God gave us the gift of free will. But it is His Spirit that causes us to produce fruit unto Godliness and not unto corruption.

Let us review. Saul was chosen as the first king of Israel. Israel was God's chosen people. Saul listened to the voice of the people and disobeyed God. As a result, God rejected Saul as king. Samuel, the prophet, was told to go to

Jesse's house and that God would show him who to anoint as king. Samuel thought that certainly God had chosen Eliab because of how he looked, but God had not. David was out in the fields caring for his father's sheep when he was called and anointed king in the presence of his brothers. The Spirit of God left Saul, and the Spirit of God came upon David. Saul was tormented by an evil spirit and needed David's help.

In these verses, we learn that obedience to God is better than following the crowd, being accepted, or receiving what others have to offer. As we move forward with the story, we will see the importance of God's Spirit and of walking in the Spirit of God.

At this point, you may be asking, "What does any of this have to do with domestic violence?" Remember, I'm setting the stage to help you understand the position of the characters in the story. I will go on to use these characters to do a parallel illustration of domestic violence. Everyone has a beginning that leads up to their story. What I did was help you understand who and where the characters were before they all met the Goliath in their lives.

Just think for a moment, what was your life like before you got with your abuser? Were you working a full-time job? Maybe you owned your own business or were enrolled full-time in college. Maybe before you met your abuser your circumstances were already horrific. You could have been rescued by him and initially treated kindly and with respect. You trusted him, only to have him turn on you and become worse to you than what he rescued you from. Whatever it was that you were doing prior to becoming involved with your partner, God saw you. Just like He saw David out in the fields caring for his father's sheep. We are God's children, and He knows exactly where everyone of us are every moment of every day. That is why, when we call upon Him, He answers.

Just as Saul, Samuel, David, and the other characters in our story made choices that changed their lives, we did also. As I previously pointed out, we have made choices in our lives that have produced serious consequences, and getting together with our abusers was one of them. *We, you and I, must own that to move forward.*

To what choice am I referring? The choice to protect your abuser. The choice you made to believe him or her after the first blow, that it would not happen again. Your choice was a choice of protection. You may not have known it then, but I am certain, just as I came to find out in my own life, that you know it now.

Am I blaming you? No. No, I am not! I am not doing what so many others in your life have done. *I am not blaming you.* So, do not put the book down and reject something that can give you the help you need. I am not in any way placing the blame of your abuse anywhere except directly with your abuser. *Your abuser's choice to hit or abuse you in other ways is not your fault.* I do not want you to feel guilty or condemned in any way.

What I do want is for you to reflect on where you were before you became involved with your partner and how the abuse has changed your life and the lives of those around you. I want you to remember a time when you had hope for your future, even if it was to get out of a terrible situation. *Remember the Hope!*

God is our hope. "And now these three remain: faith, hope, and love. But the greatest of these is love (1 Corinthians 13:13, New

International Version-NIV)." May the God of hope fill you with all joy and peace as you trust in him, so that you may overflow with hope by the power of the Holy Spirit (Romans 15:13, NIV). I invite you to pray any of the prayers below.

Prayer Point: If you have not confessed your sins before God, I invite you to do so. Say, "God, I am reading this book with a hurting heart. I am in an abusive relationship, and I feel trapped. I am fearful for my life and the lives of my children, family, and friends. I know that you sent your Son, Jesus Christ, to die on the cross for me. I believe that you raised him from the dead. Jesus, I repent of my sins. I ask you to forgive me and come into my heart and set me free. Father, these things I ask in Jesus' name, Amen.

People often say God cannot. Well, I'm here to tell you that they are wrong. God CAN do anything He wants. The moment we believe that God *cannot*, it reduces Him to a mortal man. God did come in the form of a mortal man. He came to this earth as Jesus Christ our Lord and Savior. But Jesus was fully God and fully man (Hebrews 2:5-18). Because Jesus was fully man and fully God, He, and only He, was able to die on the cross for our sins. Because He is fully God who made the heavens and the earth, He can accomplish all things. God **CAN** do anything He wants to do! What He does, or chooses not to do, is all part of His sovereign plan.

Prayer Point: Father, to the individual reading these pages I pray that you would draw him or her by your Spirit. Direct this, your child, Father, and give understanding that nothing is too hard for you. Help this your child to trust in you *by faith*, believing that you are able to, in an instant, if you so choose, to change his or her circumstances. Father, this I ask and pray in the name of your Son, Jesus Christ, Amen.

Prayer Point: Father, thank you for your Spirit that guides our lives. Thank you that your Spirit is a gift to us and is here to lead us in all truth. Help us, Lord, that we would be open to your Spirit and thank you, Father, for this revelation in Jesus' name, Amen.

Now I ask you to stay with me and read on. I believe I have a message to share with you. A message that would help to set you, and maybe someone you love, free from the terrors and torment of abuse.

Chapter 3
WHAT TYPE OF MAN IS THIS?

In 1 Samuel 17:26: we find David back home in his father's house while his three older brothers are away, deployed with Saul's army. Goliath had already made himself known to the men of Saul's army and issued his challenge. We are told that when Saul and his men heard it, they were afraid. Prior to David's arrival at the camp, Goliath had shouted his threats for 40 days and 40 nights. King Saul had promised a reward to the man who was brave enough to fight and kill the giant.

Domestic violence is like a Goliath to victims and is a blight to this nation in which we live. It is dangerous and threatening.

At some point, Jesse, David's father, told him to go to his brothers and see how they were doing. When David arrived at the camp, it was army against army, and Goliath of Gath came forward and shouted his threats once more. This time, *David* heard him. When David heard this, the Bible says, "And David spoke to the men that stood by him, saying, What shall be done to the man that killeth this Philistine and taketh away the reproach from Israel?" David was incensed. He said, "For who is this uncircumcised Philistine that he should defy the armies of the living God?"

I have two views on David's questions. One position is that David asked, "What difference does it make what happens or what reward is given for killing Goliath?" The important thing to consider is, that the giant had the nerve to defy the armies of The Living God. The text reads as if David implied that Saul's men were focused on the gain, the reward, and the money. Whereas David, on the other hand, was concerned about how Goliath mocked the God he loved.

For starters, as I think of these verses in relation to domestic violence, I think of the millions of dollars that have been poured into programs to assist victims and families and how the problem—like Goliath—still runs rampant. Maybe it is because the focus is in the wrong place. People may have become so concerned with prestige, money, and titles, etc., that they have lost their perspective or concern for the victims and families destroyed by family violence.

Maybe they are more concerned about political positions and correctness than how many children end up in the family court and state foster care systems because of domestic violence. Verses 1–3 speak of where the two armies faced off. They were situated on two mountains opposite each other, with a valley in between.

Prayer Point: Father, there seems to be such a big distance or valley between the people who are fighting the battle against domestic violence and those impacted by it. Father, I pray that the chasm between the volunteers and employees who have committed their time and energy to fight against domestic violence will be removed. I pray that agencies will unite and that barriers that enable continued suffering will be removed. Like David, we need to be more concerned about how Goliath defied you–how domestic violence destroys lives–than on the king's reward or political correctness.

In verses 1 – 11 of the Chronological Life Application Study Bible (CLASB), we receive more information on Goliath. David wore the armor of God when he went to fight Goliath. David saw Goliath's weakness, not his strength. David trusted in God's ability to defeat Goliath even before he approached the giant. Domestic violence has become like a giant in this country and other countries.

My second position is that because domestic violence has become the giant it has become, there are many who, although they are in the service industry, medical field, law enforcement, etc., do not believe that there is a solution. Also, many believe the giant of domestic violence cannot be defeated, and there is nothing big enough to destroy the giant domestic violence has become. Domestic violence has become such a problem that many are afraid of it. Like Goliath, DV is a mockery of the system of care in this and other countries. It is threatening and threatens the lives of those who come out to fight against it.

But Goliath's army and the army of the Israelites were both set on a hill, so technically, unless there was a count, both armies could look similar in force. What Goliath did was come down into the valley. He came closer to the Israelites' army so they could see his size and armor. Goliath knew that if the men of Israel saw him, they would be afraid. Batterers control their families through sheer terror. Their victims become paralyzed with fear. Like Goliath, these abusers make a big show of their strength, which is real, as is the damage they inflict and the carnage they leave behind.

Those who are already in the fight have seen the giant of domestic violence and heard all of what he has said and can do. So now they, family, friends, advocates, and professionals fear not only for the victim, children, and families, but they also fear for their own lives.

Domestic violence cannot be fought with human strength. The strength of The Living God is the only thing that will bring DV to an end! The one who goes in the name of the Lord of hosts, and Jesus Christ is His name, knows that this giant cannot stand against God. DV must be destroyed!

Chapter 4

FEAR: A CHOSEN WEAPON

If you are a helper in the service industry (law enforcement, medical, mental health, etc.), I want you to understand the spirit of fear that emanates from domestic violence. Victims are paralyzed by this fear. Like the men of Israel's army, they do not know what to do, and they are looking to you for help. David, however, having the Spirit of The Living God, understood all too well what needed to be done.

Being filled with God's Spirit, he trusted, as he had in times past, that he would defeat his enemy. The CLASB tells us that David wore the armor of God. A description of this armor is found in Ephesians 6:10-18. And there are several facts about David and his armor that I want to highlight. David had identified the enemy and understood the severity of the threat. The future of Israel depended on the outcome of this battle.

Victims of domestic violence understand the severity of the threat they face. That threat, however, is often greater than their ability to see a future without the abuser. Unlike David in our story, not all victims have a strong sense of self. Depending on how long she or he endured the abuse, it impacts their view of the future when seeking help.

David trusted in God's power, strength, and truth. He wore the breastplate of righteousness like a plate of armor and had faith that God would give him victory over Goliath. I see domestic violence as David saw Goliath, as an uncircumcised Philistine defying the name of the Lord, and it is time for it to die. Too many have died, and many more have been maimed mentally, emotionally, and physically. This giant, DV, continues to ravage our nation, and we need The Living God, His power, and His might, to take it down and destroy it.

As I read on, I read the full description of Goliath's armor. This makes me think of all the ways we describe domestic violence and what it has done. These descriptions work to put fear in the hearts of individuals who doubt that they can fight this giant. What if we didn't do that? What would happen?

Goliath was dressed to kill. His size alone could have paralyze anyone with fear. I could imagine him being over nine feet tall and the ground shaking as he approached Israel's army, stomping his feet, rattling his armor, and shouting out his challenge. As I return to 1 Samuel chapter 17, verse 7 tells us that one bearing a shield went before Goliath. His armor bearer walked ahead of him, carrying a shield. Why does a giant who is 9 ½ feet tall, wearing a bronze helmet, a coat weighing 125 lbs., brass on his legs, carrying a heavy spear and javelin, with a spearhead weighing 15 lbs. of iron, need someone to carry his shield?

The weight of the shield is not known in this chapter. It is not described. The person carrying the shield is also not described or known. I am intrigued as to why Goliath had an armor bearer. Why was his shield not described? What was the importance of this armor bearer? Was he symbolic or traditional? Was he replaceable?

As I consider the story, the mere mention of the armor bearer and the shield has significance; otherwise, why bother to mention them? As I look at this story as it relates to the giant of DV, I wonder what or who goes before it, like the armor bearer, and what is carried? Does the armor bearer, going before Goliath hold any significance to the story, as it relates to DV? Did the armor bearer precede Goliath to announce his coming? The story does not indicate that was his role. Why was the armor bearer there, and was he a distraction? If so, how?

What is it that precedes DV? What is it that warns us, distracts us, alerts us, or maybe even holds our attention so that we do not see DV for what it really is?

Just as David saw an uncircumcised Philistine defying the name of the Lord, we need to see DV as it is, destroying our families. It's possible Goliath's armor bearer was someone from a captured nation forced into slavery after Goliath had issued a challenge and defeated his nation, just as he did with Israel. What does this mean, and how would it relate to the story being told? How do those who perpetrators defeat, behave? Defeated victims behave just as Goliath's armor bearer did; they walk in silence and shame.

They tell no one of their misery, hurt, or defeat. They walk forward in life, still carrying the weight of Goliath and all he did to them, and they never say a word. It is difficult to stand up to Goliath because he always has an example of what could happen if someone did. He always has a ready victim to parade for the world to see how big and fierce he is. And, if people forget, the sight of the armor bearer reminds them of what he can do and has done in the past.

I believe the silence of victims in the past has helped DV to grow into the giant it is today. Like other social ills, public health issues, or diseases affecting humanity, we need to spread the word that there is a problem with domestic violence as well. In so doing, we alert others to the potential dangers involved. Like a disease, domestic violence thrives and spreads in silence and ignorance. And while we are silent, lives are ruined, and many are lost. If the silence and ignorance continue from one generation to the next, the disease grows in strength and intensity and develops resistance to various forms of intervention.

As a society, we must use the tools available to us to get the word out to as many people as possible. We cannot discriminate or be selective as to how or with whom we share information. Domestic violence is non-discriminatory as to the lives it destroys. No one is exempt from domestic violence. It affects every class, every socioeconomic level, every race, every gender, and every age. When domestic violence is present, no one is spared. There is guaranteed physical, mental, emotional, spiritual, or psychological damage. If we don't speak up, we ensure that the conditions under which the plague of DV spreads will continue.

If you are experiencing domestic violence, I understand it is scary to think about telling someone and seeking protection, but remember, the effects of keeping silent are scarier. Fear is one of Goliath's greatest weapons, and fear is the spirit behind DV. Everyone who has ever encountered an abuser has felt that fear. Remember, this is *not* God's plan for your life. He did not give you a spirit of fear, but of power, love, and a sound mind (2 Timothy 1:7).

Chapter 5

ARE YOU MY EQUAL? WAS I EVER YOUR EQUAL?

oth armies were camped on mountains facing each other. 1 Samuel 17:4: tells us that a champion went out of the camp of the Philistines. Goliath of Gath was his name, and verses 5 and 6 describes him. Verses 8-11, say he stood and cried out to Israel, asking why they arrayed their army against them. It was as if to say, "Why bother?" He yelled and shouted that he was a Philistine and they were servants of Saul. He did not recognize that they were Israel's army, servants of the Most-High, God, but rather identified them as servants of Saul.

People know in whose power you walk, whether you walk in your own power or in the Lord's. When God chose David and told Samuel to anoint him, Saul had just disobeyed God by not destroying the Amalekites as God had commanded him to do. So God took His Spirit from Saul and placed it on David. Obedience is crucial to God as it imitates Christ.

After Goliath taunted the armies of Israel, he challenged them to send out one man to fight him. If that man won, the Philistines would become slaves to Israel, but if Goliath won, Israel would become their slaves. After he challenged them, Goliath went a step further. He said, "I defy the armies of Israel this day: give me a man that we may fight together." The next verse says that when Saul and all Israel heard the words of the Philistine, they were dismayed and greatly afraid. Goliath set down an all-or-nothing challenge; he was not afraid of Saul. The King of Israel had lost his power, and Goliath was not impressed by him.

When I think of batterers and how they respond to laws designed to protect their victims, they, like Goliath, are unafraid and unfazed. Abusers knowingly break the law. They believe they are above the law. To them, the laws and the people who follow them have no power. Like Saul, victims cower before abusers who defy the system. Restraining orders don't always work. Police still treat victims with disdain, and the courts are often powerless to help victims. This is evident when a man can beat a woman almost to death and, in many cases, get less than a five-year sentence.

Batterers today are just like Goliath in David's day. They are loud, well protected, fearless, unintimidated, threatening, and unafraid. They shout threats that make their victims cower in fear, just as Saul and his army did. Many of today's advocates and others working in the system are like Saul and his army, dismayed and greatly afraid. I believe that this is the result of the silence. This silence has allowed domestic violence to grow in strength and potency. Lawyers, judges, police officers, doctors, senators, congressmen, and many other high-ranking officials have modified the laws to protect abusers. The system of justice is weakened in their favor.

Father, we need your strength and intervention.

Chapter 6

WHO WILL STAND AND FIGHT?

I
n 1 Samuel 17:12 – 15: we read of David and who his father was, and that his three older brothers were soldiers in Saul's army. We learn their names and find out that David was the youngest. His brothers followed Saul, but David returned from Saul's house to Bethlehem to feed his father's sheep. Verse 16 says, "And the Philistine drew near morning and evening and presented himself for forty days." So, from the time Goliath appeared with his threats and challenged them to send a man to fight, and for the 39 or 40 days following, he got closer and closer to the Israelites' camp.

Verse 16 says he drew near in the morning and evening. As I think about that Jesus, I am reminded of the torment victims face day and night. Verse 11 tells us that Saul and his men were dismayed and greatly afraid. One dictionary's definition of dismay is to break down the courage of completely, as by sudden danger or trouble, dishearten thoroughly, daunt. Another definition is to cause someone to feel consternation and distress.

When a woman or man is involved in a domestic violence situation, her or his abuser, like Goliath, breaks down their courage completely. Abusers do this by attacking suddenly and terrifying their victims. Afterwards, he taunts (teases, or threatens) her morning and evening. His threats may not be overt but may come in the form of criticism of the way she looks, of her parenting, of how she keeps the home, or of her intellect. The constant criticism, ridicule, and putdowns erode her confidence and self-esteem. Each day, he continues the emotional and mental attack against her to weaken her resolve and cause distress.

An abuser is a daunting (fearful) foe. The definition of daunt is to overcome with fear, intimidate, or lessen the courage of.

A woman in a domestic violence situation is like Saul and his men, trapped by a Goliath. Goliath had completely broken down their courage, intimidated them, and caused them to feel terrified and disheartened. The definition of dishearten is to cause (a person or group of people) to lose hope, enthusiasm, or courage; to discourage (someone) to cause to lose spirit or morale. They lost all hope. And for 40 days, he kept up his barrage of threats against them.

Verse 11, says that when Saul and all Israel heard the words of the Philistine, they were dismayed and greatly afraid. Goliath was strategic in his approach against Israel's army. But David was not there when he did all those things; David was at home, tending his father's sheep. Sometimes it is to one's advantage not to be in the midst of the crowd because we begin to think and believe as they do. Time alone, time with God in prayer, time in reflection and contemplation away from the madness of life, is good preparation for the battles of life.

Time alone with God strengthens us, and gives us confidence, power, wisdom, grace, and protection. Time with God teaches us to navigate life's challenges, dangers, mountains, and valleys. God teaches us to trust in Him.

Goliath, like all abusers, paralyzed his victims with fear and dismay. When your spirit is broken, your courage is gone, and you feel there is no hope in sight, what then is there left to do, but to become despondent, discouraged, and dismayed? The only help for those feelings is the Spirit of the Most-High God, who gives us courage and hope, delivers us from all our fears, and sets our feet on solid ground. When God is for us who can be against us?

I look back on verse 16 and read where it says for 40 days he drew near morning and evening, and I think of the woman who goes to work and is followed by her abuser, or called and harassed constantly, to see where she is.

The abuser shows up unexpectedly, wherever she might be. Like Goliath, he is in her face morning and night, a constant reminder of who he is and why she should be afraid. Imagine the mental and emotional torment of having to live with that each day. What a strain on a person's mind!

Prayer Point: God, I am so thankful for your wisdom, for the courage you have given me and will continue to give me. I pray, Father, for every woman, child, and man facing the Goliaths of domestic violence in their lives. I pray that you would send them a David, a Goliath slayer. Holy Spirit of God, manifest yourself into their hearts, minds, and souls. Teach them, Jesus, that they, like David can stand and slay the giant in their lives, if they would trust in you. Father, I believe in you for all things. I believe in your

Son Jesus Christ, who died on Calvary's cross, who prayed for me that I would be kept from the evil in this world, and who gave me the Holy Spirit to comfort and to guide me. Father, I love you and thank you for loving me. I love you, Lord. It is time to slay the giant. It's time we in America slay the giant of domestic violence and proclaim the name of the one true and Living God, and Jesus is His name.

The words Goliath spoke when he made his challenge to Israel are significant in understanding how to slay that giant. In chapter 17, starting at verse 8, we read where Goliath stood and cried unto the armies of Israel and said unto them, "Why are ye come out to set your battle in array? Am not I a Philistine and ye servants to Saul? Choose you a man for you and let him come down to me? In that same verse, the CLASB says Goliath stood and shouted a taunt across to the Israelites, saying, "Why are you all coming out to fight?" he called, "I am the Philistine champion, but you are only the servants of Saul. Choose one man to come down here and fight me."

At the start of a relationship, the two people involved are considered equal (1 Samual 17:3). Both come into the relationship with their own armies (baggage). Verse 4 says that out of the enemy camp went a champion, Goliath of Gath. And then we read about who Goliath was.

This makes me consider what happens when an abuser finally shows his victim his true colors. For victims, the first time could be as unmistakably clear as Goliath's challenge to the Israelites. Choose a man to fight me. It can also be as confusing as a push, slap, outburst, or throwing something that is later justified as not what or how it appeared. That moment can also range in intensity, with the victim paralyzed by fear or slightly confused and left wondering what just happened.

What is the lesson here? Beware of a man who is boastful and lacks humility—a man who shows off his strength. Beware of one who is quick to step out front, not to cover or protect you, but to boast and proclaim how great he is.

I also thought of the man who has false humility and puts his armor bearer out in front, using things and others to be deceptive. Goliath's armor bearer was not fully described, so he may have been the size of an average man. When others saw him, they could have assumed he was carrying the armor of an ordinary sized-man. But Goliath had a reputation. And it is important to know the reputation of any person we might become romantically involved with. Goliath stepped forward and began to shout threats and challenges to Israel's army, but before he issued the challenge, he identified who he was, who he believed them to be, and asked them why they bothered to muster their troops against him.

In a domestic violence relationship, the abuser may also start with verbal assaults and abuse long before there is actual physical violence. He lets the woman know, maybe subtly at first, that she, is the weaker one and unable to stand against him. He may come at her shouting and getting right in her face, towering over her in a threating manner. He intimidates her with his presence. His verbal attacks could also include words that make her feel like her efforts to stand against him are futile. He might let her know that family, friends, and even the law can't help her.

This is usually all done before he ever hits her or challenges her to fight him. He mockingly says she could call the law, a brother, or father, etc., and he would gladly kill anyone she calls.

Some men terrify their partners by becoming violently angry and raging, or by throwing things at them, sometimes just short of hitting them. Some abusers may walk around with weapons during arguments, or drive really, *really,* fast with his terrified family in the car. In other words, his actions are threatening, but initially he does not always hit her. This behavior is meant to establish a hierarchy in the relationship and let his victim know who is in control. It is also meant to cause confusion and induce fear. When she becomes frightened and overwhelmed, the mission is accomplished! Later, he may try to reassure her that he would never actually hurt her, and say things like, "I just get so upset sometimes," or, "I love you so much that I get so angry when you _____ (fill in the blank)."

Let's review, Goliath has spent 40 days shouting threats and insults at the Israelites. He got closer and closer and issued his final challenge. Send a man to fight me. Abusers frighten, threaten, intimidate, and terrify their victims. They create a hierarchy in the relationship and make their demands known. I refer to this behavior as positioning. Read on and find out more about how and why positioning matters.

Chapter 7

POSITIONING

1 Samuel 17:9: says, "If he be able to fight with me and to kill me then will we be your servants; but if I prevail against him then shall ye be our servants and serve us." As I think about these words, I realize how sad the domestic violence picture is in America and throughout the world. Here is an aggressor, an abuser, positioning himself in the life of a woman and distinguishing himself as an undefeated champion. He intimidates her. Then he lets her know that he is bigger and stronger. And among his people and nation, he is the best. He might even let her know how fortunate she is to have him.

Goliath spent 40 days taunting the Israelites after challenging them. But prior to this, he had identified himself to his opponents. The abuser does the same; he establishes the boundaries in the relationship. He ensures that he is the one who determines what happens and who is in charge. Boundaries in an abusive relationship usually include strict rules on what the woman can and cannot do, where she can and cannot go, with whom she is allowed to talk and whom she is not, and procedures on how things should and should not be done.

The abuser establishes *total* control over the life of his victim. Like Goliath in the valley, he draws closer and closer every day, boxing her in and isolating her from everyone and everything [that means anything] in her life. He suffocates the life out of her by controlling her actions and even, to some extent, her thoughts. She becomes hyper-focused and sensitive to every word he says while trying to anticipate his every move.

The positioning period in the relationship sets up the abuser as the champion. Because he has successfully taken this position for himself, like Goliath in the valley, he now has the freedom to move about and take control of his victim's world.

Many of you may identify with the story I'm about to tell. There are women in violent relationships who now have criminal records because they were too *afraid* of their abusers to say no. When he directed them to break the law (whether it was a moral law, or a legal statute), they felt powerless and feared for their lives. Because of their fear, they complied, and as a result, they were either caught with their abuser or caught alone and took the fall for him. Other victims were threatened with losing their children because the abuser now had illegal activity he could hold over their heads. Once the abuser positions himself within the relationship and is established as a batterer, the victim is at his mercy.

Verse 3 of chapter 17 says that both armies were positioned on opposite mountains/hills [depending on the Bible version]. The verse also says there was a valley between them. Goliath went out of his camp and down into the valley, while the Israelites stayed put on their mountain. Women in domestic violence relationships are often immobilized by the actions of their partners. They are stuck on the mountain (stuck in the relationship) and not free to move about as they please. Because Goliath was the first to step forward, he had control of the valley and probably everything in it.

Likewise, an aggressor establishes ownership and control over the woman's possessions and everything with which she is involved. Once the man establishes his position in the mind and life of the woman, he then abuses those stolen rights and weaponizes them against her. The couple may be married, in which case the law entitles him to many rights, and these rights are extended even further if children are involved.

Once the abuser establishes his position, he issues a challenge for the victim to send someone to fight him. The message is, "If I kill him, you are mine. And if he kills me, you are free." The control an abuser exerts on the mind and emotions of his victim lets her know that she belongs to him. The psychological impact of "I own you! And your only way to freedom is if I die" carries a *weight* that most victims cannot navigate or bear.

As the abuser positions himself, he uses that time to wreak emotional havoc. When Goliath first identified himself (and identified the Israelites as "servants of Saul"), he was telling the Israelites who they were, what their status was, how he saw them, and what he thought of them. In other words, he belittled the army of The Living God by calling them mere servants of Saul.

When the abuser disrespects who you are as a person, your position, place, state in life, your heritage, or even makes fun of what's important to you, these are tactics meant to weaken you emotionally. Now, no single thing, in and of itself, can be considered abusive. But a *combination* of things that tear down, intimidate, terrify, and isolate are evidence of positioning.

What about the man who does not take the time to position himself but immediately begins battering his victim? There is no warning or challenge as in Goliath's case, where he took time to wear down and terrify his opponent. When a batterer is immediately violent, there must be immediate intervention.

Just as David killed (stopped) the lion and the bear, this person must be stopped immediately. A man who begins a relationship with violent abuse is a serious threat. That man has no sense of self-control. There is no moral compass by which he is guided. And there is probably nothing anyone can do to motivate him to change his behavior. A man such as this can only be changed by the hand of The Living God! He must want that change for himself. No one can want it for him. This type of man is dangerous. He was dangerous before you met him, and he will continue to be dangerous after you are gone.

When it comes to this type of aggressor, I pray that you are not maimed for life and that you get out of the relationship alive. What you must decide is: do you leave with your life, or do you risk your life by staying and continuing to hope for change? Anyone in a relationship with a person such as this must protect themselves. Safety must come first.

Violent abusers are predators, and David prevailed over the predators that attacked his flock because he had the strength of The Living God on his side. David fought in God's strength and won on more than one occasion. David killed both the lion and the bear and recovered his sheep, and the sheep were unharmed. The understanding here is that David moved, trusting that God's Spirit was with him, and knowing that God would guide and protect him. He did not face dangerous predators in his own power. As I mentioned above, safety comes first. Do not become physically or psychologically (trying to outdo) entangled with your abuser. If violence was his immediate response after meeting you, he will not hesitate to destroy you if you challenge him.

The power of the Lord is great and mighty; like a strong tower, God is one we can run into. Psalm 34:4 says, "I sought the LORD and he heard me and delivered me from all my fears." If you are in a relationship with an abuser who attacked you immediately or shortly after you met, he or she is dangerous. **Prayer Point**: May the peace and love of God be with us.

Again, I am *NOT* advocating violence or revenge against your partner. What I am suggesting is that you put your trust in The Living GOD. Pray for guidance and preserve your safety immediately. Think of your life, and if there are children involved, their lives as well. Consider what needs to be done so that all of you survive this experience. All it takes is one blow to the head, a push down the stairs, or a kick that has too much force, and then. . .you or your child could be gone.

Chapter 8

GOLIATH WINS!

Another point to bring out from Goliath's challenge [of choose a man to fight me] is as follows: When a victim gets another person involved by asking for help and the abuser manipulates that person, he wins. If law enforcement is called and they leave without arresting the abuser, he wins. If law enforcement removes the abuser from the home without arresting him, he wins. If they lock him up and he returns to the home upon release, he wins.

Anything done to the abuser that does not stop his abusive actions is a win for him. If he wins, like Goliath's proclamation to the Israelites, a life sentence is pronounced on the victim. "... *but if I prevail against him and kill him, then shall ye be our servants, and serve us.*"

It is important to understand that any small win for an abuser is a victory. And in his mind, he now owns the victim. You may have been in an abusive relationship for decades and continue to endure the abuse. Years ago, it was believed by abusers that if they paid for their marriage licenses, they owned their wives. Yet another twisted lie that abusers tell themselves to wrongly justify their abusive actions. Abusers believe they own their victims by virtue of the win.

Once he is established as the victor, the question then becomes, "What can be done about Goliath?" Not only does Goliath now own the woman in his mind, but her immediate family as well. This becomes evident by the family's inability to successfully intervene, get the victim to leave, or stop the violence. In his mind, he also owns extended family, friends, co-workers, and anyone else with whom the victim is associated. In other words, like the giant in our story, he believes he owns the "entire nation of Israel."

So, what is the answer?

Read on because this is where I believe we are in this country. Goliath has been established and has taken control of and made servants of many nations. We are not at the beginning of this battle, nor even at the end, but in the midst of it. Goliath has roamed free for centuries, and it is time to slay the giant of domestic violence and take back the army of Israel (our lives and freedom).

Who is this Goliath?

Let's take a moment to focus on Goliath. Chapter 17:4 -7: describes Goliath in enough detail to give a visual of how he looked. Verse 4 says, "And there went out a champion out of the camp of the Philistines named Goliath of Gath whose height was six cubits and a span." When I think of these words, the description lets me know that Goliath was known in his hometown, in his nation, and among his people. His size is recorded because, in comparison to other men, he was a giant.

To a woman in a domestic violence situation, the man abusing her is a giant in her eyes. He could be a man of huge stature, physically strong and tall, or both. He could be a man of prestige and/or position, someone well known in his job, in the community, or just in the home. A woman could be protecting the image of her abuser in the eyes of her children, family, or friends.

Verse 5 says, "And he had on a helmet of brass (bronze) upon his head and he was armed (clothed) with a coat of mail; and the weight of the coat was five thousand shekels of brass (125 lbs.)." Wow, can you imagine the force and power of such a man? Think for a moment about the strength of a man who wore a coat of mail weighing 125 pounds.

I have been beaten before. I've been beaten to the point of submission and immobility—to the point of fearing for my life and passing out. When I think of the strength of Goliath, I understand the fear associated with being involved with someone who appears to be larger than life. You see, when a woman considers her abuser, she does not see him as a regular man. She sees, feels, and knows the strength in his hands and feet when he lays that weight upon her in anger. When she thinks of him, she feels, as I felt, the pain of his strength as he beats her. Goliath is unstoppable to her because he is not viewed as a person but, rather, he is felt in degrees of pain and fear. Her Goliath is a giant, strong and fierce, clothed in armor, and unstoppable.

Verse 6 says, "And he had greaves of brass upon his legs and a target of brass between his shoulders" (a target of brass is a sword, spear, and shield). Goliath's legs were covered in brass, so his legs were protected and made even heavier and stronger by the weight of the brass. When a woman has been kicked by her abuser, she no longer identifies his steps as the mere sound of feet walking towards her. What she hears as he approaches is the sound of a living weapon coming towards her.

Goliath had a sword, a spear, and a shield on his body. For the men who use weapons to beat, threaten, or intimidate their victims, they are as Goliath was. On his person, Goliath had a shield, which meant protection. If the woman tried unsuccessfully to defend herself in the beginning and the abuser overpowered her, all her defenses are gone. Goliath now reigns and continues to wreak havoc in her life. He has used and will continue to use his weapons to beat her down. His shield protects him from times when she may fight back, so his reign of terror will continue.

Verse 7 says, "And the staff of his spear was like a weaver's beam (a weaver's beam is a cylindrical wooden rod that makes up part of a boom), and his spear's head weighed six hundred shekels (15 lbs.) of iron, and one bearing a shield went before him."

When I read that his spear's head weighed six hundred shekels of iron, a picture comes to mind of a powerful arm with the hand balled into a fist of anger coming at me. Can you imagine? Can you? Can you imagine being hit by 15 lbs. of iron in the face, breast, head, or stomach? If you have been to the gym or a facility where there are weights, think of the 15-lb. dumbbell. Think for a moment about someone swinging that dumbbell at you. Imagine that much weight being swung at you in anger and with no restraint … God help you.

Prayer Point: I pray for anyone reading these words who has had this happen to them. Because I know, personally, that anger to that extreme cannot be restrained. And when you have been on the receiving end of what felt like 15 pounds of iron, the pain and fear it causes is real, *very* real (tears).

And finally, verse 7 says, "...and one bearing a shield went before him." Someone out there is aware of the abuser's behaviors. Someone out there knows what he is capable of. The one who bore Goliath's shield was, I am sure, skilled in battle and strong. Although it was not specifically stated, his job was likely multifaceted. He was there to announce Goliath's coming, protect him, defend him, or deceive the enemy. There are many who carry the shield of the abuser, and they too must be exposed and stopped *if* they seek to do you harm. For it is likely they know what Goliath (the abuser) is capable of, and they have both seen and participated in his destruction, whether by their silence or by openly defending him.

On the other hand, maybe the person knows the abuser is just that—an abuser. But they are afraid to speak up and help his victim because they may have been his victim in the past and don't want to turn the abuser's attention back onto themselves.

Another scenario involving Goliath's armor-bearer may involve the person who knows of the perpetrator's ways and warns the victim who refuses to see or believe that her abuser is really that bad.

Regardless of what the scenario is, find out about the man that you become involved with before you are hurt. If you are already in a relationship, it is not too late to find help. The mere fact that you are reading this book is an indication that you want change. My prayer for you is that you trust God, trust your instincts, and preserve your life.

Prayer Point: Father, I thank you for your revelation, and it is my prayer, Jesus, that lives would be touched and set free from the Goliaths of domestic violence all over this world. In Jesus' name, Amen.

Chapter 9
WHO IS THIS DAVID?

1 Samuel 17:17-18: gives an account of what was going on with David once he returned to his father's house. We know this because in the last verse of chapter 16, David was calming Saul by playing music on the harp. At some point, he returned home, because in verses 17 and 18, his father, Jesse, says to him, "…take now for thy brethren an ephah (65 bu = 65 bushels) of this parched corn, and these ten loaves, and run to the camp to thy brethren. And carry these ten cheeses unto the captain of their thousand and look how thy brethren fare and take their pledge."

Reading these words made me think of two things: 1.) **To victims:** As David unexpectedly showed up in the intimidated Israelite camp, you never know when help may unexpectedly arrive on your scene. It can happen. 2.) **To family and friends of the victims:** As a person connected or related to someone in an abusive relationship, you never know when you might find yourself being called on to help in a situation you may not have known existed. How would you respond if you were unexpectedly called on to help in a domestic violence situation? It is important to be knowledgeable and ready, especially if you are a relative or friend of someone you know [or may suspect] is a victim of DV.

Now David had been in Saul's home, before (we know that from chapter 16). However, they had not been in battle when David was there. But things had changed. Therefore, when Jesse sent him to check on his brothers he may or may not have known of their predicament with Goliath. As I read verse 17, I was reminded of a visit I received back when the violence against me was severe. It was an unexpected visit. And when my relative arrived at the house, she was surprised to find out what was going on.

David's father sent him to check on his brothers, and when we are in relationships, we should have people who are connected to us checking in on us to make sure we are okay. Most women experiencing abuse or violence are isolated and feel very alone. Family members and friends should provide sustenance (needed fellowship, companionship, food, help, or just their supportive presence). Jesse not only told David to check on his brothers and take them something to eat, but he also asked him to find out how they were doing.

He said to David, "...and look how thy brethren fare, and take their pledge." Two important elements of this verse are: 1.) Jesse wanted David to put eyes on his brothers, to see for himself how they were doing. 2.) He wanted David to speak to his brothers face-to-face so they could tell him how they were doing.

If someone you love is in a violent relationship, they *need* you to check on them. One of the ways abusers maintain control is by isolating their victims. Though sometimes the isolation is self-imposed by the victim out of shame or simply because of how the abuser has positioned himself in her life. Feelings of shame or fear may cause her to shy away from family and friends.

Another element that pushes victims into isolation is the constant criticism, and society's negative perception of women who struggle with domestic violence. But, regardless of whether isolation is self-imposed or otherwise, the victim still needs to be checked on. She needs to know there are people out there who care what happens to her.

Too many times family and friends avoid the victims because, in the past, they have defended or refused to leave their abusers. *But victims need their family and friends to support them.* The person in a violent relationship may not leave immediately, but knowing there is support has helped many victims leave their abusers. Victims need to know that their abusers are lying when they say, "Nobody loves you," or "You will never make it without me." When family and friends break off communication with the victim, the abuser wins. The more he wins, the more power he gains over his victim.

Being connected to someone other than the abuser [and those he approves of], can save the life of the victim. Check in on your daughter, mother, sister, cousin, friend, relative. Don't let them think for one moment the abuser might be right. Do not do it.

Verses 19-25 describe Saul and his men preparing to fight the Philistines. The battle between victim and abuser rages on at all times. There is no peace once the threats begin. There is no peace once the violence begins.

The next verse explains that David got up early and went to check on his brothers, just as his father had commanded. When he arrived, the men were arrayed for battle. Verse 21 says, "For Israel and the Philistines had put the battle in array, army against army. And David left his carriage in the hand of the keeper of the carriages and ran into the army and came and saluted his brethren."

I imagine when David got to the valley and saw that the army was pitched for battle, there was an urgency in his spirit to see his brothers and find out how they were doing. There are times when family members arrive at the residence of the victim and are immediately alarmed that something is going on that is not quite right. They sense from the moment of their arrival that there is danger. That's how it was with David. He went straight to his brothers and greeted them. David had to see for himself, just as his father had instructed him, how they were doing. Like David did, I advise you to talk to your friend or loved one yourself. Don't take the word of the abuser. Put eyes on your loved one. Make sure she or he is okay.

Talk with the victim privately. **Do Not, speak to the abuser. Do Not confront the abuser or ask him to stop if you see or suspect there is abuse going on. Do Not threaten or challenge the abuser.** If you witness the violence, get help. If you are unable to convince the victim to leave in the moment, respect her/his wishes. Find out what she/he would like you to do. Again, speak to the victim *privately.*

If you arrive at the home and the victim is bruised or has evidence of abuse, talk to the victim *alone.* If it is possible, leave the residence with the victim, but only if you can do so without confrontation.

Find out from the victim what she wants to do. Ask the victim how you can help and follow through. Educate yourself about domestic violence and how a victim responds to it. Do *not* abandon the victim. If there are children in the home, help the victim to understand the danger the children are in and the potential of losing those children. Do Not confront the abuser!

Do not leave with the victim if the children are staying behind unless she insists. If you are unable to take everyone with you, do not initiate or encourage the victim to leave if you suspect the abuser would harm the children after you are gone. Abusers are known to use children and pets as weapons to hold victims emotionally hostage. Some abusers would hurt their own children to punish the victim. So try to avoid this scenario at all costs.

The abuser's goal is control. The ultimate control over a victim is to know that she or he suffers emotionally or mentally over the loss of a child, or children. Do not give the abuser that power or satisfaction of knowing he has forever tormented his victim by taking away her child.

Chapter 10

CONFRONTATION

A s David talked with his brothers, the Bible says, "Behold there came up the champion, the Philistine of Gath, Goliath by name, out of the armies of the Philistines and spake according to the same word, and David heard them."

No more suspicion. No more doubt. When you are with the victim and her abuser confronts her, threatens her, or speaks to her in ways that leave you feeling uncomfortable, concerned, or afraid for her, your suspicions have been confirmed. An abuser who has control over his victim is unafraid of family members or friends. Abusers understand their position in the minds and lives of their victims. Make no mistake, he is not confused. His attention and concern is not about you. His focus is 100% on her.

He knows she is afraid. He knows he has control. He knows she will do whatever he says, regardless of who else may be around. His goal is to keep his hold on her, to keep her afraid and unable to focus on anything except fear of him. The presence of another person [whom he may or may not know] does not necessarily pose a threat to him, because his focus is his victim, what she thinks, what she believes, what she fears. He only has to control her ... no one else. Like Goliath did, while David talked with his brothers, the abuser will sometimes continue with the same threats, and even perpetrate acts of physical violence in front of others. Abusers are masked manipulators. They are often skilled at reading the room, sizing others up, feigning vulnerability, or showing aggression, depending on their assessment.

If you are with a victim and her abuser attacks her verbally or physically in front of you, he is doing more than trying to frighten her. If he scares you into doing nothing, he has you in his control. If he does not scare you and you leave the victim there with him, there is a likelihood that his failure to intimidate you may escalate the violence against her.

If he is the type to attack her physically in the presence of others, he would not hesitate to take her life. If he succeeds in frightening you into doing nothing, the victim may feel abandoned because you were too afraid to get involved. If, however, you leave and get her the help she needs, and that help is successful, you may have saved her life.

Be warned, however, that this type of abuser does not like to lose. The loss of his victim will likely intensify his anger against her. God's grace is the only thing that can protect you and the victim from harm.

One of the greatest fears of domestic violence victims is that they cannot be protected from their abusers. Victims know their abusers have the ability to get to them at any time. She may be driving in her car, relaxing or sleeping in her home, walking down the street, in a restaurant, or out with friends. She knows he has access to her. And that terrifies her. Because of this, many victims stay with their abusers. Paralyzing fear prevents many victims from leaving their abusers.

Why do I say it is only the grace of God that could protect you and the victim? I make that statement because I believe by faith in Christ that He is able to keep us from harm. God gives us the wisdom to make wise decisions and the courage to execute those decisions. God also promises to keep us safe. He promises that His angels are encamped around us. And, before Jesus left this earth, He prayed and asked the Father to keep us from evil. I believe that when we put our trust in Jesus Christ, and make Him Lord and Savior of our lives, He watches over His word to perform it.

His promise is that His word would not return void. The same way God orchestrated David's entry into the palace, He can also orchestrate our protection from harm and danger. I believe that, and I hope you do too.

Chapter 11

THE RESPONSE

A fter Goliath repeated his threats, 1 Samuel 17:24: says, "And all the men of Israel, when they saw the man, fled from him and were sore afraid." They retreated.

This verse makes two very important points: First, in verse twenty, we read that the armies had each armored up and arrayed themselves to advance before David reached his brothers. Second, we read that once the men of Israel saw Goliath, they panicked and retreated. Many of the men had heard his threats from a distance and had seen him from afar, but seeing him up close was different. Seeing Goliath in a face-to-face, real-time situation caused so much fear in the hearts of the men of Israel that they ran. The Bible says they were "sore afraid," which translated into "very much afraid," afraid enough to retreat before the battle had even begun.

The Victim's Response

There are many involved in the fight against domestic violence who do not understand the victim and why she behaves the way she does. They don't understand her responses to her abuser's actions, and they especially do not understand her fear.

From the onset of the relationship and that initial act of violence, that initial threat, the abuser strikes fear in the heart of his victim. Fear is the weapon he uses to immobilize his victim, just as Goliath did when he first appeared on the scene. He let Israel's army know that death was the only outcome. No one other than the victim knows how close she has come to death at the hands of her abuser. No one can understand the fear that drives her like an automaton. The only thing the victim knows, or believes she knows, at this point is that no one can save her from this Goliath with whom she lives.

Because she is so misunderstood, she is often criticized when she cringes in fear and retreats at the voice of her abuser. They do not understand that when he speaks, she jumps, or the price she pays if she doesn't. No one knows how her stomach ties in knots when he approaches. His very presence and the sound of his voice fill her with anxiety; her nerves are shot, and she becomes physically sick. She is crippled by fear and unable to respond in any way, except to retreat or do as he commands.

When she is with others and her Goliath speaks, if she defies him, the consequences will come, and they can be near fatal. This is why, when a victim attempts to leave her abuser, the violence becomes more severe and is often deadly because Goliath will not be defied. A victim facing a Goliath has to retreat if she wants to live. If she has children, retreat is inevitable, for she knows all of their lives are in danger. Retreat is, in her mind, the only way she will live to see another day. Her Goliath is a champion with a proven track record.

In the mind of Goliath, losing his victim means losing control, and losing control means being vulnerable. Goliath was probably a victim at one point in his life. To him, to be vulnerable means to be victimized, and rather than be victimized, he maintains control by victimizing others, by maintaining his position as the abuser.

The Helpers Response

The men of Israel ran for their lives when they saw Goliath. There are those who victims might turn to for help, but the ones they turn to might also be afraid of the abuser and are thus ineffective to the victim and the cause.

Some might approach the issue of DV idealistically, thinking that their education and training fully equips them to understand the situation. There is, however, a lack of knowledge, a lack of training, and a lack of understanding of the complexities of abuse. The victim is judged, and might receive help or support, based on factors that does not include her immediate needs. Those with the power and credentials to offer assistance often leave victims feeling confused, exposed, and aware that the individuals helping them do not understand the victim-abuser relationship. Many of those whom victims are most likely to turn to for help simply do not possess enough insight into the victim's world to be helpful. Others are rendered helpless and afraid when they meet the Goliath of the relationship and realize he is not intimidated by them or possible legal repercussions. When they encounter this behavior, many simply do not know how to respond.

The push of many in the system against the victim, along with the push from the abuser, places the victim in a catch 22 (very difficult position), which only serves to squeeze whatever hope she might have had out of her.

The last thing victims need are more threats from those to whom they turn for help.

Another thing that can render helpers ineffective is when they see what an abuser has done to his victim or witness, firsthand, his public behavior. Family and friends have witnessed beatings so severe victims are hospitalized. They may know of women who were maimed, burned, scarred, stabbed, or shot to death by their abusers. The list goes on and on. As the men of Israel fled when they saw Goliath, fear grips the very souls of those who might help a battered woman, and often their instinctive response is to flee.

Family and friends often want victims to do what they are oftentimes unable to do. Think for a moment, if the victim was able to get away from her abuser, work without being harassed, and start a new life without fear, depression, anxiety, etc., don't you think she would have done so already?

Helpers who have seen the Goliath in the lives of victims have retreated in fear themselves, often asking the victim to stand alone against the very giant they ran away from. A victim does not enter a relationship in hopes of being abused. Initially, she saw her partner as a man of her own size (not as a giant). However, when Goliath emerged and she was gripped with fear, she lost all ability to fight the giant in her life. So she stays on the mountain, immobilized, trying to strategize and hoping those around her will advance with her. She is often disappointed that when they finally do try to help, they become frightened, and they too retreat.

I have heard many professionals in the helping community express concern for their own safety and the safety of their families. Once they begin working with a victim and realize the Goliath she faces, fear can also grip their hearts. There is a spirit of fear, and some in the helping community operate in that spirit. It is important that those in the helping community acknowledge what they and the victims are up against.

Imagine for a moment, what if you were afraid of snakes and came home one night to find someone lying in wait for you. He kidnaps you and takes you to an unknown place and drops you into a pit full of snakes. What do you think your reaction would be? The sheer terror of the experience would probably send you into cardiac arrest. If that did not happen, you would probably go crazy from the mental and emotional trauma. If, and I do say, if, you made it out alive, you would forever be traumatized by that event. A diagnosis of post-traumatic stress disorder would best describe your actions and responses going forward. Well, oftentimes, domestic violence is to the victim what the snake pit is to the one who is terrified of snakes.

Chapter 12
THE RAVAGES OF FEAR

here is a difference between normal fears that help keep us safe—for example, fear of snakes, scorpions, rabid dogs, or black widow spiders—and an unnatural fear because someone is tormenting our lives.

In 2 Timothy 1:7: the Bible says, "For God hath not given us the spirit of fear, but of power, and of love, and of a sound mind." When we walk in fear, we are powerless to overcome the challenges we face in our lives, because fear hath torment. But ". . . perfect love casteth out fear. He that feareth is not made perfect in love." Despite what the abuser and victim say about their love for each other, the truth is, it is not love. He torments her and she is afraid of him, that is not love.

Second Timothy 1:7 says God gives us a sound mind. A woman tormented does not have soundness of mind because she is distressed.

Many, *many,* women who are victims of abuse could be diagnosed with PTSD. Many self-medicate and find unhealthy ways to calm the storm within their minds because of the sheer terror. They fail to make sound decisions concerning their own lives and the lives of their children because of feeling dismayed. They put their futures, their bodies, and their lives in danger because they dread what saying no to their partners would mean. Many have no power over their own bodies and are prostituted, exposed to sexually transmitted diseases, or forced to have abortions because they are afraid of their abusers. Some women, as mentioned earlier, are involved in the criminal justice system because of their abusive partners.

Love does not torment. First Corinthians 13:4-8: says, "Love is patient, and kind, love is not jealous, boastful, proud, or rude. It does not demand its own way. It is not irritable, and it keeps no record of being wronged. It does not rejoice about injustice but rejoices whenever the truth wins out. Love never gives up, never loses faith, is always hopeful, and endures through every circumstance. Prophecy and speaking in unknown languages will become useless, but love will last forever (CLASB)."

It is especially important to say something about these verses. There are many different translations of the Bible. In the King James Version, love is referred to as charity. No matter the translation, it is important to understand the meaning. There are women and men who read these verses and say to themselves "I do love my abuser," and they may, but love casteth out fear. Some may strive to meet the qualities outlined in these scriptures, thinking that the more they demonstrate these qualities the less often their abuser will respond abusively.

No matter who you are or where you are at this moment, understand that many women have suffered needlessly trying to love a man into changing. Love, like anything else, is a choice, and the actions abusers take are their choices.

Yes, they can help themselves. Yes, they can STOP hitting you. Yes, they do not have to act that way. And yes, they do know what comes over them when they hit you, despite what they may say.

No matter how much love you may pour into a person, that love is ineffective if the person refuses to accept it. You may walk perfectly in God's love, and your abuser may still beat you to death—or near death because it is not you; it's him.

Your life matters to the God who wrote those scriptures about love because that's the way He feels about you. God wants you to know *that* kind of love, He wants you to experience it, enjoy it, bask in it, and live in it every day of your life. He never meant for you to be tormented by fear. He never meant for your children, family, or friends to be tormented by fear. God wants you to know, feel, and be loved.

Open your heart and stretch out your faith. Open your mind and stretch out your hand to God, today. Say yes to a love that is gentle and kind and keeps no record of wrong-doing. Say yes to God and a love that is not jealous, irritable, boastful, or proud. Say yes to a God who will patiently love you back to wholeness and health and bring you into his everlasting peace. Say yes to Christ Jesus!

Verse 25 of 1 Samuel chapter 17 takes a different turn in this saga and is almost like a bridge, but not quite. We see a shift in the focus and attitude of the men of Israel. Verse 25 states, "And the men of Israel said, Have ye seen this man that has come up? Surely to defy Israel has he come up: and it shall be, that the man who killeth him, the king will enrich him with great riches, and will give him his daughter, and make his father's house free in Israel."

Wow, this verse really speaks of women who have reported of those [they have worked with] who promised them so much if they would leave their abuser. When the men of Israel asked the question, "Have ye seen this man that has come up?" they acknowledged Goliath's presence and his stature. Just one verse earlier, they had fled from his presence signifying to him that they were helpless and afraid. When some in the helping community confront or are confronted by the abuser and they retreat, they shift their focus from holding the abuser responsible for his actions to holding the victim responsible. This approach, however, re-victimizes or does not take the needs of the victim into consideration. Victims are sometimes pressured into taking legal action before they are ready. This tactic often fails because they fear both their abusers and any negative repercussions.

Victims are often promised many things without consideration of the risk. The benefits are highlighted, but the dangers are left unmentioned. Just as verse 25 promises riches, women are promised help, financial assistance, and housing. The verse further promises the king's daughter; and women are promised the possibility of another man who will treat them right. The truth is, no one knows if you leave your abuser whether or not you will end up with another man who will treat you right. Only God knows your tomorrows.

Finally, verse 25 promises to make his "father's house free." The last sentence, more than any other in this verse, speaks volumes of truth, and that is where I place my attention. Please know, that though the story speaks of killing Goliath, that is NOT what I am suggesting. No one has the right to kill another human being, circumstances permitting. When I refer to the destruction of Goliath, as in the last sentence in verse 25, I speak of the part that says, "making his father's house free."

When Goliath no longer controls your life, when fear no longer permeates your heart, mind, soul, and spirit, then and only then will you be free. The Goliath in your life has to be destroyed (legally, morally, and physically stopped from abusing you) in order for you and your entire house, family, and friends to be made free.

The men of Israel understood that the only way freedom could come was through the destruction of Goliath. Who then, would be brave enough to stand up to Goliath when those who came to fight fled at the very sight of him? Who in the victim's life is brave enough to stand up to Goliath and say no more? Now that those sent in to help have run away in fear, who will take up the charge and help you stand against the giant in your life?

Prayer Point: Father I thank you for your guidance. I pray for every woman, man, or child who reads this book. I pray for the hearts that ache with pain so great it is felt physically within them. I pray for families torn apart by abuse and violence and for children who are confused and cowering, afraid for their mom or dad.

I pray for the mothers and fathers whose daughters and grandchildren are trapped in abuse, and feel helpless and afraid. Father, I pray for strength; I pray for peace. And I pray for safety for my readers. Father, I pray that everyone who opens the pages of this book will accept your love, your protection, and your strength. I pray that he or she will allow you to heal their heart and bring them to the point of wholeness and forgiveness. I pray, Father, that they will learn to trust in and rest in you, allowing your peace to wash over them like a river of warm water. Let them know, Father, that your love is real. Let them know that your love is true and that you care for and love them. In Jesus' name, Amen. I love you, Lord.

Chapter 13

DESIRING CHANGE: UNDERSTANDING THE MEANING OF FREEDOM

I spoke of a shift in the previous chapter and that shift is clearly visible in 1 Samuel 17. Verse 26 says, "David asked the men standing near him, What will be done for the man who kills this Philistine and removes this disgrace from Israel? Who is this uncircumcised Philistine that he should defy the armies of The Living God?" (NIV)

For the first time in this story, someone explores the possibility of what happens if Goliath is no longer in the picture. David wanted to know what Saul said would happen to the man who killed Goliath. There were three promises made to the one brave enough to face and defeat the giant. First, the king would reward him with great riches. Second, the king would give him his daughter to marry, and third, the king would make his father's house free in all of Israel. Can you imagine how life would be transformed for the man brave enough to kill Goliath? Not only would he immediately become wealthy, but he would also become royalty, and his family will be given a noble rank.

In desiring change, there comes a time in your relationship when you will get tired, tired of the threats, the abuse, the yelling, and the fighting. During this time, you will become open to the possibility that things can be better, that you don't have to accept the unacceptable. When this happens, you will begin to pursue other options. This is where I want to introduce you to Jesus.

There are many directions I could take this story, but the one direction that is most profitable is the direction that leads to the salvation story. The parallel between the king's promise to David and God's promise to us is remarkable. Before continuing I want to clarify that when I consider the rewards of killing Goliath, I refer to killing the fear and *not* your abuser. I pray I've made that abundantly clear. This book does not condone or recommend violence of any sort.

Why do I focus on killing the fear in your life? Because the moment a victim is directly or indirectly exposed to or experiences domestic violence, fear begins to take root in their life. The longer a victim remains involved in the abuse, fear is rooted deeper, and its hold becomes more and more difficult to break. A new giant has appeared on the scene, and its name is Fear. I say a new giant because the *fear* to which I'm referring, is different from being scared or even afraid. This fear grips every part of your being, and I would even say it goes down into your soul.

The Bible tells us in 2 Timothy 1:7: "For God has not given us a spirit of fear, but of power and of love and of a sound mind." The spirit of fear associated with domestic violence does the exact opposite. It strips us of our power, promotes hate of self and others, and causes us to feel like we are losing our minds. This spirit tries to imitate God, in that the victim begins to believe that their abuser is everywhere, when in fact, it is the spirit of fear. Removing the fear from your life will bring you lasting change. Keep reading to find out how.

The first promise was that the king would reward David with great riches. God promises us peace that passes all understanding---not the peace the world gives but the kind of peace that He gives.

The peace God offers is a lasting peace that is deep and Holy Spirit inspired. This kind of peace helps us to deal with life's most challenging situations without coming apart at the seams, self-medicating, or feeling like we are losing our minds. The peace God offers settles our troubled hearts and allows us to know that God is greater than the situation or circumstance. God's peace equates to and far surpasses the wealth and riches offered by the king. Accepting God's peace delivers us from fear, and once you accept God's peace into your heart and mind, it will become a part of your very existence and permeate every part of your life—your home, job, and family.

I highlight God's peace in relation to the promised riches of the king. When a king bestows something on someone, it is known and acknowledged throughout the realm. When we accept God's Spirit, then power, love, and a sound mind are bestowed upon us. We have peace with God because His precious Holy Spirit brings us into all truth. All the promises of God become ours.

The kings second promise was, ". . . and he will give him his daughter." God's promise to us is that if we accept His Son, Jesus Christ, we will have everlasting life. The king promised to give his daughter to the man who killed Goliath, and that man would no longer be alone, he would have an immediate companion, a wife, for the remainder of this life. God's promise to us is that if we accept His Son, He will never leave us or forsake us and that He is with us always, even unto the end of the world.

God, who is the King of Kings and Lord of Lords, gives us a guarantee of Jesus' presence and the Holy Spirit's guidance and direction in our lives. The king's offer in David's day is no comparison to God' promises, and I do not make that comparison. There is only one God who can make the promises of eternal life and lasting peace. Accepting Jesus Christ is better than anything you will ever receive from mortals. God's promise of His Son brings comfort and peace by faith.

The king's third promise stated, ". . . and makes his father's house free in all Israel." Can you imagine going from being a subject in a kingdom to immediate royalty and what that would mean? But not only would you receive that gift, but so would your parents, children, brothers, sisters, and everyone else in your immediate family. Wow! The destruction of fear (Goliath) in our lives and the acceptance of Jesus Christ, sets us free. And as we live a life for Christ, His influence impacts our entire household. God's promise says, "For God so loved the world that He gave His only begotten Son that whosoever believeth in Him should not perish but have everlasting life" (John 3:16).

Another one of God's promises says, "If the Son therefore shall make you free, ye shall be free indeed" (John 8:36). Wouldn't you like to be free? Free from fear, free from torment, free from anguish, enjoying the peace of God which passes all understanding, knowing that God will never leave you or forsake you? How wonderful would that be? Trust in His promises. Believe Him by faith. And accept Him by faith.

Second Corinthians 1:20 says, "For all the promises of God in Him are yea and in Him Amen unto the glory of God by us" (KJV). Another version says, "For all of God's promises have been fulfilled in Christ with a resounding yes and through Christ our Amen (which means yes) ascends to God for His glory. Every promise God has ever made, He fulfilled in His Son, and that is why Jesus tells us no one comes to the Father except through Him.

Looking back at our story, even if Goliath was destroyed and the person was made rich by the king, that person was not made royalty, and his house was not made free, until he received the king's daughter. We too are made free when we accept God's Son. We too become wealthy in God, through Christ, and are given the gift of salvation and eternal life. We also receive the promise of His Holy Spirit living within us and guiding us into all truth. Truth that will set us free, wisdom to govern our lives, peace that surpasses all understanding, and power to stand strong. God is all-knowing, but He allows freedom of choice and free will. Just like in the biblical account, not every man in our story accepted the King's challenge to destroy Goliath. Likewise, not everyone who hears the good news of Christ accepts His promises.

Our choices govern our lives and God's love for us allows us the freedom to make those choices. Accepting Jesus is a choice made by faith and one only you can make. God is patient and kind; his love waits for you.

In the second part of 1 Samuel 17:26, David says something we had not heard from any other soldier in Israel's army. Not only was David asking about the promise of the king, but he was also concerned about who Goliath was and the position he had taken against Israel. The second sentence says, "For who is this uncircumcised Philistine that he should defy the armies of The Living God?" David was like, "Wait, okay, I understand what the king says he will do for the man who kills this giant, but more importantly, who does this giant think he is? Where does he get off thinking he has the right to come against the army of God?" Israel was God's chosen people and to defy His people was to defy God.

David called Goliath uncircumcised because God's chosen people were circumcised and set apart for God. God took care of his people. He went before them in battle, and he protected them from their enemies. David's question to the men around him showed his interest in the king's promise but also his disgust with Goliath's unmitigated gall in challenging God's army.

There are many who are disgusted by the abuser when they see his control over the victim's life. and how victims cower in fear at the sound of the abuser's voice. Just as the men in Israel's army cowered.

Family and friends might take the position [that David did] of, "How dare you think that you can talk to her or treat her that way? Who do you think you are?" Unlike the men to whom David spoke, he knew God's ability to defend his people, and David did not fear Goliath. Because David was not afraid, he had an immediate advantage over the other men. Unlike the rest of Saul's army, David was focused on God's ability and not on the size [or threats] of the giant who stood before them.

Verse 27 says, "The people answered him after this manner saying so shall it be done to the man that killeth him." This confirmed to David that what he had heard was true. The king would reward the man who defeated the giant. There are many things spoken about who Jesus was and who Jesus is. But the Bible tells us that Jesus is God in the flesh. It further tells us that Jesus is God's Son and the only one who can forgive our sins and offer eternal life.

Jesus is God! He knows exactly who you are, where you are, and what you need. Call on Him, talk to Him, and He will answer you. God is a very present help in times of trouble; He is the lifter up of our heads, and a strong tower into which we can run. God loves us beyond anything we can even imagine.

God provides us with a love that fills our hearts, minds, spirits, and souls. His love is truly mind-blowing and the best thing you will ever experience!

The reason God's love is so wonderful is because the Bible tells us that God *is* Love! Don't let questions and doubts persuade you not to trust and believe in Christ. Take that leap of faith by saying, "God, I believe that you exist; show me that way; lead me to your Son, Jesus Christ, who died for my sins." Help me to trust in, believe in, and accept Him as my Lord and Savior. Forgive me of my sins, and lead me along the path of righteousness. Amen.

God hears, God sees, and God knows. Trust that He has heard your prayers and has forgiven you and accepted you as His child through faith in His Son, Jesus Christ.

In the previous chapter, we see a shift in the tone of the story as the desire for change becomes evident. We begin to read where other options are being explored and thoughts of removing the giant are considered. There will come a time in your relationship, when you begin to entertain the idea that things need to change. For some, it will happen early on in the relationship. It might happen after finding out you are pregnant or after the birth of your child. It may happen as a result of the loss of a child, or hospitalization, or some other tragic event. For others, the thoughts of change will come much later, when you can no longer live with the abuse and you're just plain tired.

It might happen when you're too tired to go on [with things the way they are] and you're too tired to quit. You just want the abuse to stop! You want the fear to go away, and you want to live a peaceful and quiet life. You are mentally, physically, and emotionally exhausted, and you want it all to stop. But you don't know how to make it stop.

David presents as a person who also wants change. Although David had not been among the men when they advanced towards the enemy, he heard how the giant had spoken to them. He heard the Giant's threats to enslave the entire nation. David knew that this could not be allowed and was not what God desired for His people. What the giant proposed was unacceptable. It was time for change.

Change, however, does not come easy, and, at times, may come at an extremely high price. Not everyone is open to change. Many resist change. There are those who become physically and verbally violent in order to stop change from happening. And the people in your life who are going to oppose you as you try to change, may also use violence to stop you.

When David began to inquire about what Saul would do for the man who killed Goliath and to voice his opinion about what he thought of Goliath's threats, his words were not welcomed by all who heard them. Verse 28 shows evidence of this:

> 1 Samuel 17:28: says, "When Eliab, David's oldest brother, heard him speaking with the men, he burned with anger at him and asked, Why have you come down here? And with whom did you leave those few sheep in the wilderness? I know how conceited you are and how wicked your heart is; you came down only to watch the battle." (NIV)

David is confronted by his own brother—not one of the other men but his own flesh and blood. Do not for one minute believe that your desire for change will be accepted by everyone closest to you, because it may not.

David was anointed king in front of his brother Eliab. Eliab's reaction to David may have stemmed from envy, jealousy, or anger. You may have family members who try to convince you not to leave, or that things are not as bad as you think they are. However, these family members don't live with you, and they are not tormented by fear as you are. Therefore, only you can decide if you want to live with abuse for the rest of your life. You have a choice; yes you do! This is your life!

First of all, your abuser will be your biggest opposition. He will not want you to leave the relationship, stop the abuse, or get help. You are not your abuser's first priority, except to keep you under his control! Your abuser is interested in satisfying himself. *He* is his main concern.

God will give you the courage, strength, and most importantly, the wisdom to leave your abuser *safely*, if that is your desire. You do not need to touch a hair on his head or harm him in any way.

In Romans 12:10 the Bible says, "Dearly beloved, avenge not yourselves, but rather give place unto wrath: for it is written, Vengeance is mine; I will repay, saith the Lord." In another place, it is written, "It is a fearful thing to fall into the hands of The Living God."

My prayer is that as you read this book, you will come to the knowledge that you do have a choice. And my prayer is that you will choose life. Jesus Christ died for you that you would have life, and life more abundantly. Even if you don't choose Jesus, still know that you have the right to choose to live.

The first part of verse 28, tells us that when David's brother, Eliab, heard David speak to the men, his anger burned at David. The very fact that you speak of leaving an abusive relationship will arouse anger in some people. That is why it is better not to speak about your plans to *anyone*, unless it is with someone who is helping you prepare. Many victims have been sold out by family or friends sympathetic to the abusers, and you are never in so much danger of losing your life as when you are leaving the abuse.

As I mentioned before, your abuser will be your biggest opposition and his anger against you will increase. It is true that the most dangerous time for a woman in an abusive relationship is when she tries to leave. Think of your abuser's anger like a fire raging out of control. I don't say this to scare you but to caution you and make you aware that even the talk of leaving will ignite the abuser's anger. There are others who may also become angry when you talk of leaving. They may be someone close to you, someone you love and thought you could trust. Depending on the age of your children, you may face their anger as well. Anger is oftentimes a result of fear. Family or friends may become angry because you talk of leaving. They may be afraid for you and terrified of your abuser.

Although it will be difficult, try to understand their position. Remember, they are afraid of the same person you are, or they fear for your life. If this is someone you trust, whom you can hold in confidence, talk with them, and help them to understand your decision. It may take some time between making the decision to leave and actually leaving. If you are determined to leave, be careful and work with trusted people who will encourage and support you.

Eliab asked David two questions: Why are you here and with whom did you leave the sheep? Have you ever tried to pour your heart out to someone and the only question they can ask is "Why are we talking about this?" Eliab reminds me of such a person who has missed the point or whose focus is only on himself. Eliab also reminds me of the person who verbally attacks the victim by putting them down. When Eliab sneered at David by asking him who he had left his sheep with. He minimized the importance of David's responsibilities at home.

Like Eliab, there will be people in your life who are critical of your choice to leave. You will experience rejection and resistance from those who are in positions to assist you and refuse. But don't lose heart. Eliab could have supported David's decision, but instead, for his own selfish reasons, he chose to criticize and question him, to ridicule him in front of others.

Eliab said to David, "I know how conceited you are and how wicked your heart is; you came down only to watch the battle."

Expect accusations and rejection. Expect some people to throw your past in your face and even threaten you in some ways. Expect your abuser to threaten to take your children or to report you to child protective services or some other government agency. Expect him to do whatever is necessary to keep you powerless and in the relationship. If you decide to leave, do NOT speak of leaving to anyone except someone you trust implicitly. And expect resistance.

Back to our story. At this point, David had not made any decisions. All he had done was ask about the king's promise and expressed disgust with the giant's threats against God's people. All you have to do is speak of change or question your current situation, and you could experience the same kind of malicious response that David got from his brother. What's crucial to remember at this point is that if your heart and mind question your current situation, it is time for change.

Chapter 14

THE POINT OF NO RETURN

Let me review where we are because, after this, there is no turning back. The children of Israel are facing a giant who threatens to kill any man who fights him and to enslave their entire nation. The giant frightened the men. And tormented them with his threats for 40-days.

Like Israel, you are faced with an abuser who beats you, threatens you, (and probably your children as well), torments you, and (may) promise to kill you. He has caused fear in your heart and in the hearts of those who love you. You may feel trapped. The abuse has gone on for too long (any abuse that goes on longer than the first time has gone on too long), and you are tormented by fear.

The entrance of David into the story represents change. David was in the camp and heard what Goliath said at the very time the men of Israel had arrayed themselves to advance against the giant. Goliath repeated his challenge, as he had done so many times before, and the men of Israel cowered before him. David was surprised and disgusted. Then the men of Israel said to David, "Have you seen Goliath?" And they told David what the king had promised to the man who killed the giant.

This is a pivotal point in the story that I do not want you to miss. David did something that changed his life and the future of an entire nation. Although David was disgusted when he heard the giant's challenge, he was interested in the promises of the king and wanted to know if they were true. David had two choices: either listen to Goliath's threats or listen to the king's promises. David chose to listen to the words of the king.

There may come a time when someone will hear how your abuser talks to you or see how he treats you and tells you there is a better way. There will come a time when someone tells you of the love of Jesus Christ, the King of Kings and Lord of Lords, of his love and his promises. This point in your life will be a crossroads where you will have to make a choice, just as David did. And, for you, that choice will be: Do you continue to believe the things your abuser tells you, or do you listen to and find out if the promises of God are true. Once you hear of God's love and his promises, will you verify, as David did, if what is being said is true, or will you continue to live in fear of your abuser.

Understand that no matter what you choose, when you first hear of Christ, it is not the end unless you give up. The love, mercy, and grace of God is never ending. If you hear of Jesus and don't accept Him the very first time, God will not reject you. Keep what you hear inside your heart, and when you are ready and the time is right for you, call on Jesus, and he promises He will be there for you. Roman's 10:13: says, "For whosoever shall call upon the name of the Lord shall be saved."

The name the Bible speaks of here is the name of Jesus Christ. God promises to save you when you call upon the name of his Son. And remember, the promises of God are yes and yes! When you make the choice to listen to the promises of the King rather than the threats of the giant, your life will never be the same.

Prayer Point: Father, I pray for every person who reads this book, that the mustard seed of faith, that you have placed in all of us, will grow in their hearts. I pray that this reader's faith in you would begin to blossom and produce fruit. I pray that this reader would call upon your name and trust you to be set free. Help your child to know and understand that freedom sometimes starts in the heart and mind, believing that change is possible. Give your child hope, give your child strength, give your child courage, Father, to believe that change can happen. Comfort your child, wrap your arms of love around your children and give them the knowledge and wisdom they need. In Jesus' name, Amen.

David's oldest brother did not appreciate David's presence in the camp, and he made it very clear how he felt. Eliab accused him of doing something wrong. But David knew something Eliab did not; David knew his rights, and his response to Eliab [in verse 29] tells us just that. David responded to Eliab by saying, "What have I now done? Is there not a cause?" David's response tells us two things: 1.) He did nothing that his brother could accuse him of, and 2.) His presence there was justified.

What David knew that Eliab did not, was that he was sent by his father to check on his brothers. He was sent to check on the very man who accused him of wrongdoing and of having wrong motives. God sent his Son, Jesus Christ, into the world for all of us. David also knew, once he got there and heard and saw what was going on, that there was a need for him to be there. After all, he asked Eliab, "Is there not a cause?"

When you begin to hear about Jesus and begin to ask questions, or you even begin attending church, expect that there will be those who will question what you are doing. But just as David asked his brother, is there not a cause? Remember, God sees your pain, your hurts, and your needs. He knows you have a cause. And God sent Jesus to help you. He sent Jesus to be there for you, for in Him, you will find safety.

Is there not a cause?

Don't be the one to reject, resist, or be angry at Jesus, as Eliab was with David. Eliab was broken and afraid, tormented by fear, and unable to think clearly. Try not to make the same mistake about Jesus that Eliab made about David. Try not to make final judgments about Jesus without truly taking the time to find out who he is.

David stood up to his brother because he knew he was not wrong. I pray that God would give you the courage to stand up to those who try to keep you trapped in abuse and keep you from accepting Jesus Christ as your Lord and Savior.

After standing up to his brother, David turned away from Eliab and asked some of the other men if what he had heard about the king's promises were true, and they told him yes; what he heard was true. As you hear others talk of Jesus Christ, pray and ask God to fill you with his Holy Spirit, which God promises will lead you in all truth. God is faithful and wants you to know the truth about Jesus Christ. Truth is sometimes hard for victims of domestic violence to face, but trust God, and He will not let you down.

1 Samuel 17:31: says; "And when the words were heard which David spoke, they rehearsed them before Saul, and he sent for him." David had

been asking around about the king's promises, and word got back to Saul. When Saul found out that someone in the camp was inquiring about his offer, he sent for David.

When I thought of verse 31, I was reminded of several scriptures but two specifically, John 6:44 and John 12:32. The first, John 6:44: says, "No man can come unto Me (Jesus) except the Father who has sent Me draw him: and I will raise him up at the last day." And the second, John 12:32: also says, "If I (Jesus) be lifted up from the earth I will draw all men unto Me."

When we begin to inquire about the things of God, just as David asked about the words of the king, God is drawing us to Himself. The interest we have comes from a desire for something better: a better life, better understanding, peace, better finances, or whatever is currently lacking. That is what we seek to improve. As God begins to draw us to Himself, our desire to know Him increases, and He draws us closer and closer to His Son. James 4:8: says, "Draw near to God, and He will draw near to you." David knew that Goliath's opposition to God's army was wrong. He also knew that Goliath's threat to enslave God's people was wrong.

So, when David heard the King's offer, his interest was piqued. David investigated what he had heard, and eventually ended up in the presence of the King. As you seek God, He will draw you to Himself. And the closer you get to God, the closer He will get to you. That is one of His promises. And as I pointed out before, God's promises are all yes and yes.

Numbers 23:19: says, "God is not a man that He should lie, nor the son of man, that He should repent, has He said, and He will not do it? Or has He spoken, and will He not make it good?" In another version, it says, "God is not a man so He does not lie. He is not human, so He does not change His mind. Has He ever spoken and failed to act? Has He ever promised and not carried it through? (CLASB)." Titus 1:2: says, "…God cannot lie…."

There is a statement that I have made many times in conversations past, and that statement is that oftentimes people blame God for things that others do. Don't blame God for the choices someone else has made or for what someone may have done to you. Do not reject God because of another person's bad choices. Do hold them responsible for their own actions. Just as I encourage you to exercise your free will, I want you to understand that your partner also has free will. Your partner chose with his own free will to abuse you and those you love. God did not make him do what he did.

God is not a man! It is by faith that we believe God, and without faith and believing in God, none of His promises matter.

For example, Hebrews 11:6: says, "But without faith it is impossible to please Him (God): for he that cometh to God must believe that He (God) is, and that He (God) is a rewarder of them that diligently seek him." It takes faith to believe that there is a God. God is pleased by your faith. And when you believe in Him and seek Him in faith, He rewards you according to His promises.

David knew God and God's promises, and that is why, when he heard the giant speak, he was immediately annoyed, disgusted, and wanted to take action against him.

There is a very powerful scripture in the Bible that says, "What shall we then say to these things? If God be for us, who can be against us? (Romans 8:31)." When you, by faith, trust and believe in God, there is nothing and no one who can come against you without having to go through God to get to you.

God is, always has been, and always will be our greatest protection—hands down. Have faith! God only asks for you to have faith the size of a mustard seed, and He will grow your faith in Him. God loves you and always will. Take a step of faith and allow God to embrace you. Draw close to Him and He will draw close to you. He loves you that much because "God is love" (1 John 4: 8).

Chapter 15

TAKING THE STEPS TOWARDS FREEDOM

We open this chapter and find that David is standing before the king, 1 Samuel 17:32: says,

"And David said to Saul, let no man's heart fail because of him (Goliath), thy servant will go and fight with this Philistine." Saul's response to David was, "Thou are not able to go against this Philistine to fight with him; for thou are but a youth and he a man of war from his youth."

Goliath had been fighting from the time he was a boy, Why? Maybe he was raised to be a warrior, or maybe things had happened that forced him to become a fighter, and being a giant had only added to his ability to win. Regardless of why he fought from such a young age, he had a history of being a soldier; could David win against such a skilled person? In Saul's eyes, David faced an opponent he could not beat, but the army needed a volunteer, and David was it.

Up until this moment, David had been asking the men in the camp about what the king had promised to the man who killed the giant. David was confronted by his brother and stood up to him. He continued to investigate if what the king said was true, and word got back to the king about it. Some of you have heard others talk of Jesus and God, and you've wondered about it. You may have attended church or watched Christian programs on television. You may even have a Bible that you've opened and read or thought of reading. But up until this point, that is all you've done.

When Saul sent for David, David was faced with many choices. He could question why the king wanted to see him. He could resist going and be forced to appear before the king, or he could have pretended that he was not the one inquiring about the king's promises. David's choices at that moment were numerous, and so are yours. *You have choices.* Despite what you may have been told by your abuser or others, you do have choices.

What David did, however, was accept the invitation of the king and gladly appeared before him. God has been drawing you to Himself because He wants you to accept Jesus, as your Lord and Savior. Change requires action. When the king called for David, he went willingly. God is drawing you, calling you to accept His Son. Will you do it?

A step cannot be taken without movement. Taking a step towards God takes faith, accepting Jesus Christ takes faith, and change takes faith. Choose to go before the one true King of Kings and Lord of Lords, and you will find all his promises are true. Accept the gift of His Son, who freely gave His life for you that you may live and be free.

Romans 10:8-13: says, "But what does it say? The word is near you; it is in your mouth and in your heart, that is, the message concerning faith that we proclaim: if you declare with your mouth, "Jesus is Lord," and believe in your heart that God raised him from the dead, you will be saved. For it is with your heart that you believe and are justified, and it is with your mouth that you profess your faith and are saved." (NIV)

Take the first step towards your freedom; accept God's invitation when he calls you. Confess with your mouth that you believe He raised Jesus from the dead and call upon the name of the Lord Jesus to set you free.

God promises in John 8:36: "If the Son therefore shall make you free, ye shall be free indeed." God wants you to accept His Son, Jesus Christ, because God knows that Jesus has the power to set you free from all your fears. Psalm 34:4: says, "I sought the Lord, and He heard me, and delivered me from all my fears."

God knows that Jesus has the power to heal you in every way that you are broken. In Psalm 147:3: we read, "He healeth the broken in heart and bindeth up their wounds." God is a God of comfort, according to 2 Corinthians 1:3-4: These verses say, "Blessed be God, even the Father of our Lord Jesus Christ, the Father of mercies, and the God of all comfort; Who comforteth us in all our tribulations that we may be able to comfort them which are in any trouble, by the comfort wherewith we ourselves are comforted of God."

Your life is important. You are important to God. Accept the King's invitation just as David did with Saul. Allow the King of Kings, Jesus Christ, into your heart, and He will set you free.

Prayer Point: Father, I thank you for revelation and wisdom, for showing me the way I should go, Jesus, when I call upon you I trust by faith that what I am reading about you is true. Thank you, Father, for your tender mercies and loving kindness every morning. I love you Lord. In Jesus' name I pray all things, Amen.

Chapter 16

THE GIANT SLAYER

W e have reached the part of our story where David is standing before the king. As we previously read, he said to the King, let no one lose heart because of the Philistine, I will fight him. Wow! David is going to fight the giant. Imagine the weight that must have been lifted off the shoulders of the king when David made his announcement. Imagine the relief the other men must have felt when they heard someone had stepped forward and agreed to fight the giant.

As a victim of abuse (emotional, physical, mental, financial, sexual assault, no matter the type), do you sometimes wish for a champion, someone who will come to your rescue and stand up to the giant [or giants] in your life? Do you long for someone to step forward and say, "I will fight for you and protect you from whomever you fear? Are you hoping for a David?

If this describes you, you need look no further. Many years ago, before you or I had conscious thoughts, the Father and the Son decided that we should not worry. He said to us, "Let not your heart be troubled; ye believe in God, believe also in me" (John 14:1). The first thing David said to King Saul was, "Let no man's heart fail because of him (Goliath)."

David knew that fear paralyzes. So, he wanted to encourage the king and his men. When Jesus went to the Father, He wanted "all" humanity to know that He was their giant slayer and that because of Him, we had no reason to fear. Jesus promised He would fight our battles for us, and He told this to His Father the same way David told King Saul he would fight Goliath.

Why did David offer a statement of comfort to the king before saying he would fight the giant? David did so because he knew that when someone is afraid, that person's ability to make right decisions and judgments are disrupted. David wanted King Saul to know there was no need for the men to be afraid. Remember how David spent time in the camp talking with the men? He knew how they felt and what they thought. He also either saw or heard of their retreat when they first advanced to fight. And then he saw Goliath . . . the giant.

It was as if David was saying to Saul, "Trust me, you need not be afraid." Then David told the king, "Thy servant will go and fight with this Philistine." The king and his men had been on that mountain for a long time, and for the first time since the two armies faced each other, someone had finally agreed to accept the giant's challenge. David wanted to put an end to the torment, humiliation, and threats. He wanted the giant dead. David had seen enough. He had heard enough, and he knew it was time to take action. David was about to slay the giant.

Now that David had made this bold statement that he would fight Goliath, King Saul was concerned. Saul was concerned that David, who was just a young boy, wanted to fight Goliath who had been fighting since he was young. Saul did not believe David would be a match for Goliath. Just because he wanted to fight, didn't mean he could win.

David had to prove himself. He had to prove to the king that he had the ability to fight Goliath. Saul looked at David's size, then he looked at the giant, probably wondering how this boy could ever win a fight against such a foe. But David told Saul of how he defended his father's sheep when a bear and a lion took lambs from the flock. David went after the bear and the lion, killing them. In doing so, the lambs were rescued, and the threat against the rest of the flock was eliminated.

When it comes to believing in and trusting Jesus Christ, many are like King Saul, they want Jesus to prove himself. They want to know that Jesus can "Do" what He says He can do. They want to know if there is action behind Jesus' words.

The truth is that Jesus' words and the words of the Bible have always been followed by the ultimate action. John 3:16: says, "For God so loved the world (you, me, and everyone in it) that he gave his only begotten Son that whosoever believeth in him should not perish but have everlasting life." God followed his Word with the greatest act of Love ever known to humanity. He sacrificed his Son so we would not spend an eternity tormented by fear, death, and hell.

David was a shepherd, and he understood the dangers he and his flock faced. But for the love of his father and of his sheep, David watched over the flock and protected them with his life. Jesus did [and continues to do] the same for us. Jesus is a shepherd, and once you accept Him as your Lord and

Savior, you become part of His flock. And for the Love of His Father and His love for us, He gave His life to protect us from all the dangers we will face.

Like David, Jesus is not pleased when one of His lambs [or sheep] is threatened or harmed. Like David, Jesus will fight on your behalf to protect you. John 10:11: says, "I am the good shepherd, the good shepherd giveth His life for the sheep." John 10:27-30: says, "My sheep hear my voice and I know them, and they follow me. And I give unto them eternal life; and they shall never perish, neither shall any man pluck them out of my hand. My Father, which gave them me, is greater than all and no man is able to pluck them out of my Father's hand. I and my Father are one."

Once you become a part of God's family, you are protected by God and by the promises of Christ. God will not allow anyone to take you out of his hand, not as long as you choose to stay with Him. God's love for us is so great. He explains just how much in Romans 8:33-39, where Paul wrote: "For I am persuaded, that neither death, nor life, nor angels, nor principalities, nor powers, nor things present, nor things to come. Nor height, nor depth, nor any other creature shall be able to separate us from the Love of God which is in Christ Jesus our Lord."

God covered it all. He has clearly stated that there is nothing that can separate us from His love once we accept Christ as our savior.

It feels good to know there is safety and security and that fear no longer has to dominate our lives. It feels good to know that we are not alone. God is ever present. God's love for you does not start when you accept Christ as your Lord and Savior. God's love for us has been in place since before the foundation of the world.

If you read this book to the last page and decide that Jesus Christ is not who you want to commit your life to, then God the Father, Jesus Christ His Son, and His Precious Holy Spirit will still love you, and there is nothing you can do about it (1Corinthian 13, Romans 5:8, and 1John 4:19).

1 Corinthians 13 says the following about love: "Charity (love) suffereth long, and is kind; charity envieth not; charity vaunteth not itself, is not puffed up, Doth not behave itself unseemly, seeketh not her own, is not easily provoked, thinketh no evil; Rejoiceth not in iniquity, but rejoiceth in the truth; Beareth all things, believeth all things, hopeth all things, endureth all things. Charity never faileth."

Take a few moments and consider the actions of your abuser. Does he treat you kindly? Is he easy to provoke? Does he celebrate or rejoice in the truth?

Chapter 17

GOD NOT I!

So, David explained to Saul how he went after the lion and the bear that took lambs from his father's flock. He pointed out how killing both predators protected the rest of the flock from danger. But not only his flock was protected; through his heroic actions, David protected the entire territory.

How did he do it? How did a young boy like David kill a lion and a bear? How is it that he stood before the king proclaiming that he would fight Goliath of Gath, the champion of the Philistine army?

David had hope, David had faith, and most importantly, David trusted in God Most High. He trusted in God because he spent time with God and knew that God was a protector of those who trusted Him. In 1 Samuel 17:37, David said: "Moreover, The Lord that delivered me out of the paw of the lion and out of the paw of the bear, will deliver me out of the hand of this Philistine." And Saul said unto David, "Go and the Lord be with thee.

When Saul asked David how, being just a boy, he thought he could fight and win against a giant, David told him. David knew his strength and skill was more than mere natural ability. David knew that it was God's protection and covering over him, God's spirit upon him, and God's wisdom in him that allowed him to be victorious over the foes he fought. David was counting on God to provide him once again with the same spirit of wisdom, covering, and protection during his fight with Goliath. You see, David knew his God was a faithful God who never fails. If God delivered him out of the paw of the lion and the bear, then God would deliver him out of the hand of Goliath.

David was not focused on Goliath's record and all his past accomplishments. He did not care how tall Goliath was or how big or heavy his armor was. David did not care if men cowered when Goliath opened his mouth. Why? Because he knew that despite all of Goliath's fame and success, God was not on Goliath's side. David knew who was on his side. God, the creator of the universe, the creator of all humanity, the creator of all living things, was on his side.

David knew God! David said in the 23rd Psalm, "The Lord is my shepherd; I shall not want. He maketh me to lie down in green pastures: he leadeth me beside still waters. He restoreth my soul: he leadeth me in the paths of righteousness for his name's sake. Yea, though I walk through the valley of the shadow of death, I will fear no evil for thou are with me, thy rod and they staff they comfort me. Thou prepares a table before me in the presence of mine enemies; thou anointest my head with oil; my cup runneth over. Surely goodness and mercy shall follow me all the days of my life; and I will dwell in the house of the Lord forever."

David knew God! He trusted God, and he also knew that Goliath had taunted, threatened, caused fear in the hearts of, and defied the armies of The Living God. God was not pleased with Goliath.

Like David, every woman, man, boy, or girl who is faced with a giant that appears larger than life, who is threatening, terrifying, is violent, and abusive, must trust God for the wisdom, courage, strength, and His Spirit to defeat this enemy.

When you accept Christ and are filled with His Spirit, you receive peace to be free from fear, the courage to stand strong, and the wisdom to know what you must do to defeat the giant. God is able to rescue you from the hand of the enemy when you put your trust in Christ Jesus. Allow Christ to fill you with His Spirit, and let God fight all your current and future battles. As God was with David so he promises to be with you, and God keeps His word.

Chapter 18
MOVING FORWARD

David received the king's approval and his blessings. Saul told David, "Go and the Lord be with thee." Saul, wanting David to win in battle against Goliath, did what he could to help prepare the boy for battle. 1 Samuel 17:38-39: says, "Then Saul gave David his own armor, a bronze helmet, and a coat of mail." David put it on, strapped the sword over it, and took a step or two to see what it was like, for he had never worn such things before. "I can't go in these," he protested to Saul, "I'm not used to them." So David took them off again. (CLASB)

People will try to tell you how you should handle your situation, and you may think that is what I am trying to do in this book. Well, I am not. What I am doing is letting you know that a relationship where you are filled with fear is one that causes torment, stress, emotional, mental, and psychological damage. These are universal responses for anyone in violent relationships. My purpose for writing this book is to help you understand that God, who created you, did not intend for you to live in fear. God tells us in Jeremiah 29:11: "For I know the plans I have for you, says the Lord.

They are plans for good, and not for disaster, to give you a future and a hope" (CLASB).

My purpose is to introduce you to Jesus who is able to guide you and give you peace, strength, and courage to do whatever you and God decide is best for you. God wants you to have hope. He wants you to believe in a future that is bright and prosperous. God loves you and wants to teach you and show you what true and pure love really is. He wants you to live.

My purpose is to let you know you have an advocate in Christ. Jesus will come alongside you because, with Him, you are not alone. My purpose is to help you understand that there is another way and there is *"Life After Domestic Violence."* Accepting Jesus Christ as your Lord and Savior is for your benefit and your eternal salvation. Everyone in a violent relationship who accepts Christ does not always leave their abuser. Some choose to stay, and some choose to leave. Whether you stay or whether you leave, that's a decision only you and God can make together.

No matter what choice you make, my purpose is to let you know you're not alone. God loves you, and He proved his love through the death of his Son, Jesus Christ. God sent Christ to die for you because He loved you and has loved you from before the beginning of time. When you are weak and in despair, feeling lonely, or afraid, God is with you, even when you fail to acknowledge his presence. My purpose is to let you know that God wants you to know that He loves you and that He cares.

As you move forward towards destroying the enemy of domestic violence in your life, God is and will always be your greatest source of help, protection, and strength. Just as David could not fight the giant in Saul's armor, so you cannot fix your situation the way someone else fixed theirs. Pray and ask God for direction, then trust Him to protect you as you take action and move forward, just as David did.

God knows exactly how, what, when, where, and why about your future. He knows who you need to bring with you into the future He has planned for you. Trust Him, just as David did. God loves you, and He will protect you. He will also teach you and educate you on how to protect yourself. Trust Him, His Word is true!

When Saul accepted that David was serious about fighting Goliath and gave his approval, he made a very important statement. Saul told David, "Go and the Lord be with thee." I don't want you to miss the most essential piece of this story. David was confident he could fight Goliath because of his faith in God. David was confident in approaching the king to let him know he would defend Israel's army and nation because of his faith in God. David killed the lion and the bear because of his faith in God. And David would move forward and destroy Goliath because of his faith in God. David was confident in everything he did because he knew that God was with him. David knew that he could stand against the giant as long as God was with him.

As you move forward "Go and the Lord be with thee."

Chapter 19

CHOOSING YOUR WEAPONS FOR BATTLE

A s we return to the story, 1 Samuel 17:40: says, "And he took his staff in his hand, and chose him five smooth stones out of the brook and put them in a shepherd's bag, which he had, even in a script (his wallet), and his sling was in his hand, and he drew near to the Philistine."

After David met with the king, told him he would fight Goliath, tried on the king's armor, and saw it would not work, he moved forward with his plan. David did not spend much time (according to the scriptures) debating about what armor he should wear. He made up his mind, trusted that God would be with him, got the king's approval and blessings, and was ready to go.

Once you accept Jesus Christ as your Lord and Savior, trust that God will be with you. Trust that God is able to deliver you from the fear and torment you feel inside. Trust that God will give you peace.

Once you trust God it does not matter whether you decide to leave or stay; there will be a battle. And in order to be successful in battle, you must decide on your weapon of choice. For David, God directed him to choose five smooth stones out of the brook. He had his staff, his bag, and his sling. For some victims of abuse, the weapon may be departure and the need to travel light. Like David's, your situation could be a matter of life and death, and you may not have the time or resources to pack and leave with everything you own. If fleeing emptyhanded with your identification, your life, and your children is what you must do, then do it. And God will see you through.

Your situation may call for you to find a safe place for you and your children to go. You may be required to have the abuser removed from the home. You may have to face him in court through separation and child custody proceedings or through a domestic violence criminal trial. You may have to walk the long journey of receiving child or spousal support from your abuser. Some of you may decide to stay and walk in God's protection while you continue to live with your abusers. Whether you leave or stay, God is able to keep you.

Once David chose his weapons for battle, the verse says, he drew near to the Philistine. Facing an abuser is never easy. Being in his or her presence may evoke fear, stress, tension, anxiety, and or a host of other emotional responses. But with God's help, you can find the courage to stand your ground, regain your voice, and take back power and control over your life.

For some, that courage is instant, like it was for David. For others, the courage and time to face your abuser would come later. Yet, still for others, although the courage is there through Christ, you may never have to see them again. As you accept Christ, trust Him, pray, and ask Him to lead, guide, and show you what to do.

There are many in the domestic violence community, believers and non-believers alike, who will take issue with the previous two paragraphs. Some might ask, are you suggesting that victims "stay and pray?" While others might argue that I seemingly dismiss the covenant of marriage and advise victims to leave. First, not every violent relationship is comprised of spouses. Second, there are no one-size-fits all, answers for every instance of spousal abuse or domestic violence. Though there are similarities in every case, each case is also unique, with differences as well. In this book, many scenarios and options will be discussed.

In Chapter One, I told a story that marked the end of my relationship. And I remember God teaching me a very important lesson about *Free Will.* It was after the final act of violence. I went to God and made these statements and asked this question. You are God. You created the Universe. Why didn't you stop him from hitting me? The Lord woke me up in the middle of the night with a scripture I had never read before.

He led me to Jeremiah 13:23: "Can an Ethiopian change his skin or a leopard its spots? Neither can you do good who are accustomed to doing evil." I was broken, and I cried. But I knew God was saying to me, he is not going to change. I had to make a choice. Do I stay, or do I leave? I chose to listen to the voice and Word of God. God wants to speak into your situation the same way He spoke into mine. Will His words to you be the same as His words were to me? I don't know. And your decision to stay or leave is between you and God.

If this is all new to you and you have never prayed before, start by being honest, and by acknowledging God. Let Him know that you believe He is God. Ask God to forgive you for not acknowledging Him and for trying to do everything on your own. Ask Him to help you and acknowledge that God sent His Son, Jesus Christ, to die for your sins, so that you might be saved. Confess your sins to God, accept Jesus Christ as your Lord and Savior, and ask Him to fill you with His Spirit and power. Then, thank God for hearing your prayer and saving you.

Ask God for what you need from your heart. Only you know your situation. Talk to God and tell Him what is going on with you. Express to God your feelings, your fears, and your needs. Pray for your children. Understand that you are in a battle for your life (with your abuser) and for your soul now that you have given your life to Jesus Christ. For there is an enemy even worse than Goliath who wants to keep you from loving God.

Hell is real, and Satan is real, and as Goliath was to David, so is Satan to us. Anyone who accepts Christ as their Lord and Savior becomes an enemy of Satan. But just as David dealt with Goliath, Jesus defeated Satan, and Satan has no power or control over you unless you give it to him. Jesus is your shield and protection. Now that you know that, focus on building your relationship with Him, and He will show you the way.

The story continues, "And the Philistine came on and drew near unto David; and the man that bear the shield went before him." As you move forward, your abuser will confront you if he has the chance, and he may or may not be alone. Others, who know your abuser may also try to convince you that your choice to better yourself, or your desire for change, is wrong. Remember, the decision is yours, and you do have a choice.

Verse 43 says, "And when the Philistine looked about, and saw David, he disdained him; for he was but a youth…," Once your abuser sees your desire to change, or suspects that you are planning to leave, he will not like it. If he finds out that you are going to church or counseling, he will begin with criticism, intimidation, belittling, or even violence. The goal is to maintain the status quo, which is you in the home and him in charge.

When you accept Jesus Christ as your Lord and Savior, you *will* change. Your thoughts *will* change. The way you feel about things *will* change. The places you used to go *will* change. Your desires *will* change. Be prepared. Your abuser will not like the changes he see in you and will begin to belittle you just as Goliath did with David. Remember, your abuser wants to control you, he wants things to remain just as they were before you accepted Christ. It's easy to go back, but is it worth your life?

Your abuser will do everything in his power to make you afraid so you will abandon your efforts to change your situation. Some famous lines abusers use when their victims attempt change, or if they suspect their victim wants change are:

- No one wants you.
- No one will ever love you like I love you.
- You are fat, ugly, stupid, etc.
- If you leave me I will kill you, myself, and everyone around here.
- You can go, but my children or things stay here.
- No one wants a woman with a child or children.

These are just some of the statements abusers use to keep their victims cowering and afraid.

Another famous line is: You can go but not before I beat the _____ out of you (or some other threat).

Your abuser may have had years of practice perfecting his ways. He knows how to manipulate you and others to get his way. Your abuser is a very good liar and con artist. His skills of deception are very good. Be cautious; you know your abuser better than anyone else when it comes to your situation. If telling your abuser, you are leaving (and it probably will) places you in more danger than usual, don't say anything. Placing yourself, your children, or your family in danger is not something you want to do. As I said before I will say it again here; the most dangerous time for a woman in a violent relationship is when she attempts to leave.

Keep your mouth SHUT if it means saving your life, the lives of your children, and the lives of those you love.

I am going to use a scripture here to make a point. In this scripture, Jesus is teaching about giving and prayer. He said in Matthew 6:3: "But when thou doest alms, let not thy left hand know what thy right hand doeth." What this verse is saying is that when you give to the poor, don't broadcast it to everyone so you are recognized, but give from a sincere heart. God, seeing what you have done in secret, will reward what you have done openly.

I suggest that you treat your situation in the same way it is suggested in the Bible. Don't let others know what you are doing. Move in secret (in faith), and God who sees that you trust Him to help and protect you, will take care of you. If you think that someone will broadcast what you are doing to your abuser, putting you and your children in danger, do not share with that person. Listen to me, the person who you choose to share with has to love you and your safety more than they love what they think you should or should not do. Also, if you think your abuser will threaten the person you share with, don't share your plans with anyone other than God.

Goliath had one goal and that goal was to destroy his challenger and enslave the nation of Israel. Your abuser will not want you to leave, and he will not want things to change. If he allows change, he loses power, and abusers do not want to relinquish power and control.

1 Samuel 17:43: says, "And the Philistine said unto David, Am I a dog that thou comest to me with staves (sticks)? And the Philistine cursed David by his gods."

Abusers are master manipulators. When belittling fails to work on a victim the abuser will try to turn the tables and play the victim. The abuser will act as if what a victim is doing is somehow harming him. This is yet another tool in the abuser's tool kit and another way to keep the victim psychologically and emotionally confused.

Know your abuser; Remember what a master manipulator he is. You have seen and experienced him in action. The same way your abuser turns on the charm, he could quickly fly off the deep end, filled with anger and rage.

Verse 44 says, "And the Philistine said to David, come to me, and I will give thy flesh unto the fowls of the air and to the beast of the field." Goliath let David know what he thought, how he really felt, and what he intended to do to him. Goliath went from belittling David when he first saw him, to playing the victim, and finally to threatening his life. Does any of this sound familiar? Has your abuser acted the same way? Has your abuser gone from belittling you, calling you names, to crying and saying how much he loves you, to how much you are hurting him, and then, finally, to threatening you with death?

No wonder you are often conflicted and confused. No wonder you do not know whether to defend yourself, cry with your abuser, or run for your life. The truth is, your abuser is just that, abusive. And whether he chooses words, his fist, intimidation, or threats, it is all abuse.

Goliath was what he was. He was Goliath of Gath, champion of the Philistines. His size and his voice were intimidating. His mission was to conquer different nations and enslave their people. Goliath was a giant and a killer! You and only you can decide if the Goliath in your life is one you can live with or a giant you must destroy by getting him out of your life. The way you destroy the giant of abuse is to take away his ability to hurt you and to control and manipulate your life.

You know the giant with whom you live better than anyone else. Is he the kind who has no regard for life, yours, his, or anyone else's? Or is he the kind of abuser from whom you can safely escape? It is important to know the type of person your abuser is because it will determine your course of action. Yet, no matter how you choose to move forward with your decision to change, you are not alone. God is with you. God, the creator of the universe, who knows you and your abuser, can provide you with guidance on what you must do.

To some, this may sound trivial, simple, or just plain foolish. But to those who know God's power and his ability to rescue from unbelievable situations, my statement is as real as your hands that hold this book, and your eyes that read these words. God is every bit as real as you and I are.

And He has the ability to provide you with the help and protection you need to change your life. The choice is yours. Will you trust Him today? Remember, whether you stay or leave, you will need courage to face the giant. My prayers are with you.

I love you, Lord. To you, Lord, I give all the praises. Thanks be to God the Father, Son, and Holy Spirit, forever and ever. Amen.

Chapter 20
ANOTHER CROSSROAD

C hange is a process that involves a series of steps, some small and some large, some forward and some backwards. Change involves letting go of some things and embracing others. Change requires truth, acceptance, self-assessment, self-evaluation, education, and work. Change may involve recognizing self-destructive behaviors and patterns, seeking and asking for help, and accepting that you cannot make this change alone. Change takes time. For some people, the change they experience is instantaneous, and for others, it is gradual.

Change may require you to swallow your pride and open up about your situation to trusted sources. It may also require you to admit that you are broken (emotionally or in other ways), and in need of help. Change does not have to be scary or hold negative connotations. Change does not have to be approached with fear and apprehension. Change, like anything else in life, will become what you make it.

Change takes dedication, commitment, and determination. Change is not always easy especially when you are coming out of a difficult situation, but change is possible. Every good and every bad thing that has ever happened to you is locked away in your mind. Every scary and evil thought is locked away in your mind. Every moment of joy, peace, and happiness you've experienced so far is locked away in your mind. And for every person who has ever walked the face of this earth and wanted to change, the journey to change started in their minds.

You see, God, in his infinite wisdom, knew that the storehouse of our memories, emotions, feelings, etc., is in our minds. Our thoughts lead to what we believe and eventually to what we do. In Romans 12:2: God gave us an answer to help us as we move forward with change.

> "And be not conformed to this world but be ye transformed by the renewing of your mind that ye may prove what is that good and acceptable, and perfect will of God."
>
> The CLASB puts it this way, "Don't copy the behavior and customs of this world, but let God transform you into a new person by changing the way you think. Then you will learn to know God's will for your life, which is good and pleasing and perfect."

Change is possible! God also tells us in Proverbs 23:7: "For as he thinketh in his heart so is he."

Your abuser, either in a single act of extreme violence against you or in a series of violent acts, convinced you that he would ultimately kill or seriously harm you. It took time for him to establish your thoughts about the powerful position he now holds in your mind and life. Over time, some of you began to believe that you are nothing, that you are worthless and deserve the treatment you received. You aren't, and you don't. You are afraid of making decisions, going places, or even talking to people, because of what your abuser might do.

Think about it, your abuser changed you by changing the way you think, believe, and act. Change happens to us every day, and the time has come to decide which direction you will go from here. Yes, you are at yet another crossroad in your life. Each time you reach a place such as this, you will be required to choose.

I know you may not be accustomed to making decisions. You may have been made to believe that your decisions cannot be trusted. You may have convinced yourself that you cannot make good decisions, or you would not have partnered with an abuser. You may have rehearsed in your mind, more times than you can count, the terrible things your abuser said to you, like when he called you stupid, idiot, dumb, and much, *much*, worse. Maybe, before you got together with your abuser, you had been told that you would never amount to anything, and you believed it—so much so, that you decided that you're really not smart enough to make good decisions.

Whether this is true or not, a decision has to be made. Understand that to choose not to make a decision is the same as making a decision. Trust your instincts, try to remember who you were before your abuser got hold of your mind. God promises to never leave you or forsake you, and He will walk with you through each stage of your change. He will be with you when you succeed, and He will be with you when your success seems out of reach.

God will sit with you when you can't decide. Talk to Him. Let Him know that you are afraid. He knows it's been a long time since you've been on your own or made many decisions for yourself. Up to this point, He has protected you, even when you made wrong choices. Ask God for wisdom, guidance, and continued protection.

James 1:5: in the CLASB says, "If you need wisdom, ask our generous God, and he will give it to you." God has both prepared and made available to you everything you will ever need. His Son, Jesus Christ, holds the key to your everlasting peace and protection.

I realize that abusers distort the Words of God for their own benefit and evil intentions. If your abuser has used the Bible, The Word of the Living God, and Jesus Christ to justify his abuse. To you I say this, God cannot lie! Go to God for yourself. Read the Bible for yourself. Pray and ask God to give *you* wisdom, revelation, and direction from his Word.

I guarantee you that you will recognize many contradictions between what the Word of God says and what your abuser has told you. You will also find many contradictions between what your abuser does and what God's Word says he should do. For example, in 1 Corinthians 14:33: we are told, "For God is not the author of confusion but of peace, as in all the churches of the saints."

If your abuser uses the Word of God, guilt, or shame to keep you broken, beaten, confused, and in bondage, the time for change has come. You did not come across this book by accident. You're reading of this book was intentional and guided by divine intervention. Don't allow your abuser to convince you that your desire for the abuse, disrespect, and tormenting fear to stop is not God's will.

In Jeremiah 29:11: God says to you, "For I know the thoughts that I think toward you, saith the Lord, thoughts of peace, and not of evil, to give you an expected end." The CLASB says it this way: "For I know the plans I have for you, says the Lord, they are plans for good and not for disaster, to give you a future and a hope." If your abuser's thoughts toward you, actions, intentions, and plans for you are not the same as God's, do not allow yourself to be fooled any longer into believing that your abuser is doing what he is doing in the name of God. Your abuser is acting from his own selfish desire to dominate you. God's plan for you is to love you and to help you. God gives you peace, not confusion and torment.

God is the master of all change. Allow God to lead you into a changed mind, heart, and attitude. Jesus Christ changed the world over 2000 years ago, and He still possesses the power to change you if you will let Him. God has an answer to your every need. Allow Him to reveal the truth you need in your life. Change is possible! God has brought you to this place at this time. He has seen your tears and heard your cries, and through this book, He is letting you know that He hears you and He is waiting for you to accept Him into your life.

I pray you will choose to change this day, in Jesus' name. I love you, Lord. Thank you, Father, for your life-changing words.

Chapter 21

HOW TO STAND

I n our last chapter, we talked about change because you are at a critical juncture in your life. Before that, we saw how Goliath belittled David, and then played the victim, and finally threatened David with death. David was face-to-face with Goliath because he followed through with his decision to fight the giant. David knew God before he heard Goliath's challenge against Israel's army, before he went before Saul and accepted the challenge, and before he chose his weapons of war.

David's decision was complete. And as verse forty stated, he drew near to the Philistine. There was David, face-to-face with Goliath of Gath. What would David do? In 1 Samuel 17:45, David tells us what he did and how to stand against the giants in our lives. Verse 45 says, "Then said David to the Philistine, Thou comest to me with a sword and with a spear, and with a shield: but I come to thee in the name of the Lord of Hosts. The God of the armies of Israel whom thou has defied."

Can you picture this scene in your mind? David was a boy (the Bible called him a youth, tall and strong maybe, but no match for a giant) who stood before Goliath of Gath, who was wearing full armor and carried a sword and a spear. David had his staff, five smooth stones, his shepherd's bag, and his sling. He had just been threatened with death by Goliath and his response was, "I come to thee in the name of the Lord of Hosts, the God of the armies of Israel, whom thou has defied."

What confidence! David knew in his heart, in his mind, in the depths of his soul, and with every fiber of his being that God was strong and mighty and could not be defeated. David did not face Goliath in his own strength. He faced Goliath in the name of the Lord.

Proverbs 18:10: says, "The name of the Lord is a strong tower; the righteous runneth into it and is safe." How does someone become righteous, and walk in the name of the Lord? We are told in 2 Corinthians 5:21: "For He (God) hath made Him (Jesus Christ) to be sin for us. Who knew no sin; that we might be made the righteousness of God in Him (Jesus Christ)."

The CLASB Bible explains it this way, "For God made Christ, who never sinned, to be the offering for our sin. So that we could be made right with God through Christ."

When you accept Jesus Christ the Son, God the Father accepts you. When you are in Christ, you are protected and covered by God. God becomes your strong tower into which you can run and be safe. You can confidently walk in the name of the Lord, for in that name there is safety, protection, and healing. God is not only a strong tower, "He is Strength, He is a shield." When David prayed in Psalm 28:7, this is what he said: "The Lord is my strength and my shield, my heart trusted in him and I am helped, therefore my heart greatly rejoiceth and with my song will I praise him."

David knew he could not face Goliath in his own strength. But he knew that facing and fighting Goliath in the name of the Lord would mean victory for Israel's army. David trusted God in his heart, and God helped him to win. David walked confidently into the presence of King Saul to accept the challenge to fight the giant, and then he walked confidently onto the battlefield to confront the giant.

David trusted in the name of the Lord, and he walked in the name of the Lord. He faced one of the greatest fears of his people in the name of the Lord. "The name of the Lord *IS* a strong tower; the righteous runneth into it, and is safe." God's promises were true when David trusted Him, and His promises are still true today.

When we trust in God through Christ, that strong tower provides safety, rest, healing, peace, and so much more. Jesus promises this in John 14:27: "Peace I leave with you, my peace I give unto you, not as the world giveth, give I unto you. Let not your heart be troubled, neither let it be afraid."

Just imagine a life filled with peace, peace in your home, peace on your job, peace in your family, peace with your friends. But most of all, peace within your heart, soul, and mind, the kind of peace that allows you to sleep at night and wake up in the morning without fear. Jesus promises that peace and his promises are yes and yes! The only way to *stand*, and do so confidently with the peace of Christ, is to walk in the name of the Lord. God bless you. I'm praying for you.

When David walked onto the battlefield to face Goliath of Gath, he was at peace. David was not afraid, and he did not second guess his decision. David walked confidently onto the battlefield and confronted Goliath in the name of the Lord. David never stopped trusting God. Remember, your abuser is not pleased with your choice to change. Allow God to position, prepare, and equip you just as He did with David. God will guide you as you navigate interactions with your abuser. He will give you answers that address the needs specific to you and the situation at hand. When Saul spoke to David, he knew David trusted God, and he said to David, "Go and the Lord be with thee."

God gives us peace to face our fears and confidence to walk in the choices and decisions we make. The book's subtitle is "Finding My David in the Man Called Jesus," and that is exactly what I did.

When I met Jesus, I was broken, battered, and shattered. And I thought I was beyond repair. My mind was filled with fear and torment, and I was afraid of everything. I stayed afraid. One day I went to a church, not to attend the service but to get food from the food bank after I had separated from my abuser. I had two small children to feed, and I needed help.

The man at the church gave me three things after I told him a little bit of my story. One of the things he gave me changed my life forever. He gave me a bag of food, a five-dollar bill, and a book about a couple who were involved in domestic violence and whose lives were changed after they accepted Jesus Christ. After reading the book, I wanted to know more about this Jesus. My only thought, then, was that if God saved their marriage, surely, he could save mine.

This book is a testament that I found that man, Jesus, and He is true to his word. Jeremiah 29:11-13 reminds us of God's love. It says, "For I know the thoughts I think toward you saith the Lord, thoughts of peace, and not of evil, to give you an expected end. Then shall ye call upon me, and ye shall go and pray unto me, and I will harken unto you. And ye shall seek me and find me, when ye shall search for me with your whole heart."

God saw my brokenness, he knew my desire, he heard my prayers, and he answered me. Like David facing Goliath, God knew that the giants of my life were too big and too many for me to manage (face). When I met the man called Jesus, it was the beginning of the best and the greatest adventure of my life, one I am still living today.

David had a mission, and that mission was to defeat the enemy who defied the armies of the Living God. Jesus has a mission, and His mission is to let every person know that He loves them and wants them to be saved. He wants them to live in peace for all eternity, with God the Father. The Bible says this: "Beloved, I wish above all things that thou wouldest prosper and be in health, even as thy soul prospereth."

Trust God as David did, and choose to walk in the name of the Lord.

I love you, Lord. Thank you, Father, for allowing me to reach this goal.

In my next book, *Giants Beware*, I explain how to slay the brothers of Goliath. Thanks to everyone who purchased a copy of this book. Please pass on a copy to someone who would benefit from reading it. May God continue to bless and strengthen you.

BOOK REVIEWS

1. "This book is the secret weapon and blueprint that every women, person or organization can use to help others who are experiencing domestic violence. Dr. Carol Jones has put together a unique comparison of a biblical story and life's lessons to create awareness and education regarding a person's domestic violence journey. Her book is incredibly noteworthy, valuable and inspiring to help you believe in yourself, overcome challenges, increase your confidence and begin the road to recovery. "Slaying the Giant of Domestic Violence" is truly powerful! Well done!" John Formica, The "Ex-Disney Guy", America's Customer Experience Coach at www.JohnFormica.com

2. I like the parallel Dr. Jones made between domestic violence (DV) and the story of David and Goliath. The way she weaves the story and the concepts together makes it very simple to conceptualize the magnitude of DV. The way Dr. Jones went in and out of the characters and the points she wanted to emphasize regarding DV was nicely done. Overall, I feel the book is inspiring and empowering.

AP, MSW LCSW, NC